THAT MAN IS YOU!

Becoming a Man after God's own Heart

PowerPoint Presentations

Paradisus Dei

HELPING FAMILIES DISCOVER THE SUPERABUNDANCE OF GOD

A Publication of Paradisus Dei · www.paradisusdei.org

> "Be not conformed to this world; but be transformed in the newness of your mind, that you may prove what is the good, and the acceptable, and the perfect will of God.
>
> Romans 12:2

> "Faith and reason are like two wings upon which the human spirit rises to the contemplation of God.
>
> Pope John Paul II
> *Fides et Ratio*

The Tools at our Disposal

The Three Wisdoms

- The best research from secular science (especially medical and social science).
- The teachings of our faith (based upon Scripture, Tradition and the teachings of the Magisterium).
- The wisdom of the saints handed down through the centuries.

> "The Spirit of the Lord shall rest upon him: the spirit of wisdom and understanding, the spirit of counsel and fortitude, the spirit of knowledge and piety. And his delight shall be in the fear of the Lord.
>
> Isaiah 11:2-3

Becoming a Man after God's own Heart

A New Focus for Spring

- We will transition to an action orientation to implement the vision.
- We will identify the three fundamental orientations of every person.
- We will identify the three ways by which Satan tries to disrupt these orientations.
- We will see how God tries to encounter us according to these three orientations.
- We will identify seven steps to Become a Man after God's own Heart.

The Formation of the Human Person

Faculty	Formation	Excess
Intellect	Intellectual	Rationalism
Will	Spiritual	Fundamentalism

This program is desperately needed in the Roman Catholic Church today. It is the most eye-opening and rewarding program that I have ever attended! I honestly believe this course will make Catholic men better leaders of their families, which will renew the Church and change the world.

Program Participant ⊠ Texas

Small Group Discussion

Starter Questions
1. Where are you in your leadership today and how can you improve it?
2. *Who are you going to bring with you next week?*

Next Week
The Price of Failed Leadership

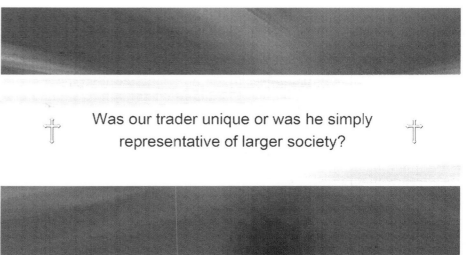

Was our trader unique or was he simply representative of larger society?

Male Sexual Infidelity

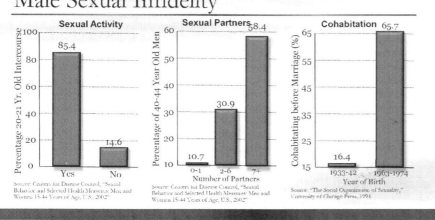

The story of King David illustrates the consequences of male sexual infidelity.

The Story of King David

- Chosen by God and consecrated as King of Israel by the Prophet Samuel.
- Commits adultery with Bathsheba, who becomes pregnant with his child.
- Arranges for the death of Bathsheba's husband, Uriah.
- Takes Bathsheba for his wife.
- Confronted by the Prophet Nathan who tells David the parable of the two men.

The Consequences for King David

1. Disharmony in the Family
"I will take your wives while you live to see it" (2 Samuel 12:11).

2. Children will Suffer
"The child that is born to you shall die" (2 Samuel 12:14).

3. Conflict in Society
"The sword shall not depart from your house" (2 Samuel 12:10).

4. Worship of God will Suffer
"David may not build a house for my name for he is a man of war and has shed blood" (1 Chronicles 22:8).

Modern men have fallen in a manner analogous to King David and greater society is experiencing the consequences foretold to King David and Israel.

Disharmony in the Family

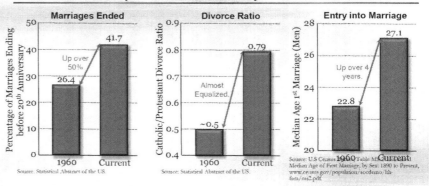

Disharmony in the Family

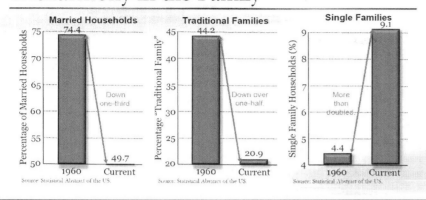

Married Households

Percentage of Married Households

74.4 — Down one-third — 49.7

1960 — Current

Source: Statistical Abstract of the US.

Traditional Families

Percentage "Traditional Family"

44.2 — Down over one-half — 20.9

1960 — Current

Source: Statistical Abstract of the US.

Single Families

Single Family Households (%)

9.1 — More than doubled — 4.4

1960 — Current

Source: Statistical Abstract of the US.

The Children will Suffer

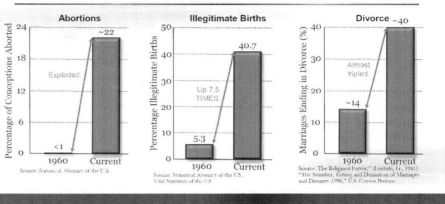

Abortions

Percentage of Conceptions Aborted

~22 — Exploded — <1

1960 — Current

Source: Statistical Abstract of the U.S.

Illegitimate Births

Percentage Illegitimate Births

40.7 — Up 7.5 TIMES — 5.3

1960 — Current

Source: Statistical Abstract of the U.S., Vital Statistics of the US

Divorce

Marriages Ending in Divorce (%)

~40 — Almost tripled — ~14

1960 — Current

Source: The Religious Factor," (Lenski, G., 1961). "The Number, Timing and Duration of Marriages and Divorces: 1996," U.S. Census Bureau.

The Children will Suffer

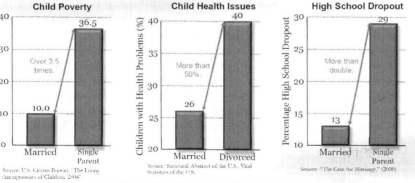

Child Poverty

Percentage of Children in Poverty

36.5 — Over 3.5 times — 10.0

Married — Single Parent

Source: U.S. Census Bureau, "The Living Arrangements of Children, 2004"

Child Health Issues

Children with Health Problems (%)

40 — More than 50%. — 26

Married — Divorced

Source: Statistical Abstract of the U.S., Vital Statistics of the US.

High School Dropout

Percentage High School Dropout

29 — More than double. — 13

Married — Single Parent

Source: "The Case for Marriage," (2000).

Conflict in Society

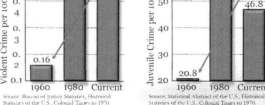

Total Crime

Crime Rate per 1000 Population

5.93 — More than tripled. — 3.47 — 1.13

1960 — 1980 — Current

Source: Bureau of Justice Statistics, Historical Statistics of the U.S., Colonial Times to 1970.

Violent Crime

Violent Crime per 1000 Population

0.59 — Up 2.5 times — 0.43 — 0.16

1960 — 1980 — Current

Source: Bureau of Justice Statistics, Historical Statistics of the U.S., Colonial Times to 1970.

Juvenile Crime

Juvenile Crime per 1000 Population

65.0 — More than doubled. — 46.8 — 20.8

1960 — 1980 — Current

Source: Statistical Abstract of the U.S., Historical Statistics of the U.S., Colonial Times to 1970.

Conflict in Society

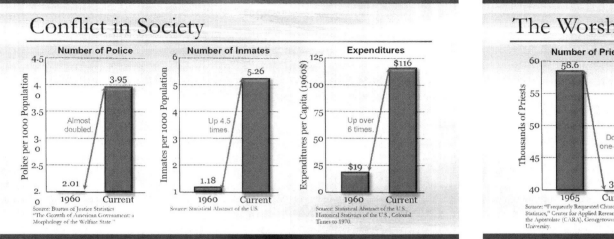

The Worship of God will Suffer

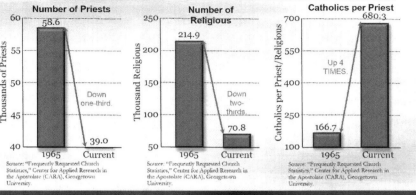

The Worship of God will Suffer

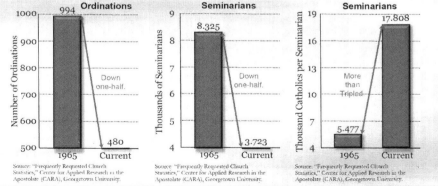

The Worship of God will Suffer

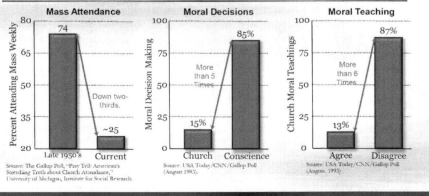

The Worship of God will Suffer

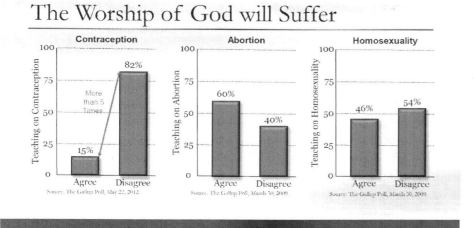

Contraception
- 15% Agree
- 82% Disagree
- More than 5 Times

Source: The Gallup Poll, May 22, 2012.

Abortion
- 60% Agree
- 40% Disagree

Source: The Gallup Poll, March 30, 2009.

Homosexuality
- 46% Agree
- 54% Disagree

Source: The Gallup Poll, March 30, 2009.

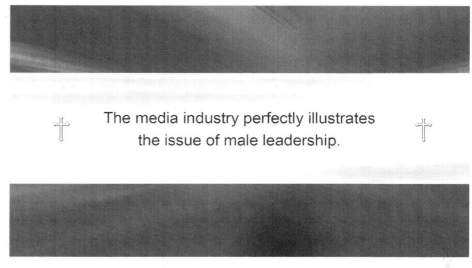

The media industry perfectly illustrates the issue of male leadership.

Leadership in the Media

- Vast majority of media elite are men.
- Over half have no religion.
- Over 85% seldom or never attend worship services.
- Nine out of ten support abortion.
- Three out of four think homosexuality is ok.
- Only 14% strongly agree that adultery is wrong.

Source: Lichter, Robert, S., Rothman, Stanley, and Lichter, Linda, S., "The New Media Elite," Hastings House, 1986-1990.

Media Consumption by Youth

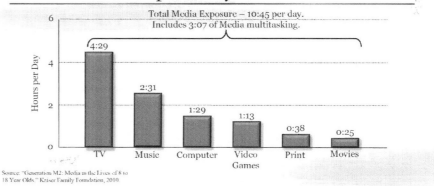

Total Media Exposure – 10:45 per day. Includes 3:07 of Media multitasking.

- TV 4:29
- Music 2:31
- Computer 1:29
- Video Games 1:13
- Print 0:38
- Movies 0:25

Hours per Day

Source: "Generation M2: Media in the Lives of 8 to 18 Year Olds," Kaiser Family Foundation, 2010.

Violence in the Media

- By age 12, typical child has witnessed 8000 murders and 100,000 acts of violence on TV.
- Approximately 70% of prime time shows and 90% of children shows contain violence.
- Nearly 40% of violence is perpetrated by "good" characters.
- Almost 40% of violent scenes contain humor.

Sources:
"Big World, Small Screen: The Role of Television in American Society," University of Nebraska Press, 1992.
Strasburger, Victor C. and Wilson, Barbara, J., "Children, Adolescents and the Media," Sage Publications, 2002.

Congressional Studies on Media Violence

- 1952: First government study on effects of TV.
- 1972: Surgeon General concludes TV violence is harmful to youth.
- 1982: NIMH – TV violence has strongest correlation to aggression of any variable.
- 1984: Study links amount of TV consumed at age 8 with adult criminal acts.
- 1986: Notel studies in Canada.

Sources:
Hoerner, Keisha L., "The Forgotten Battles: Congressional Hearings on Television Violence in the 1950's," at www.scripps.ohiou.edu/w jmcr/vol02/2-3a-B.htm.
U.S. Surgeon General's Scientific Advisory Committee on Television and Social Behavior, "Television and Growing Up: The Impact of Televised Violence," 1972.
National Institute of Mental Health, "Television and Behavior: Ten Years of Scientific Progress and Implications for the Eighties," 1982.
Williams, Tannis Macbeth, "The Impact of Television: A Natural Experiment in Three Communities," Academic Press, Inc., 1986.

Sexuality in the Media

- Sexual act or reference occurs 4 times per hour during the "family hour."
- Approximately 80% of sexual interactions are between unmarried persons.
- Less than 15% of prime time shows include fathers as central characters.
- By age 15, over 90% of males have seen both a Playboy and an x-rated film.

Sources:
Parent's Television Council, "The Alarming Family Hour ... No Place for Children."
Parent's Television Council, "Happily Never After."
1999 National Fatherhood Initiative. Strasburger, Victor C. and Wilson, Barbara, J., "Children, Adolescents and the Media," Sage Publications, 2002.

Impact of Media Sexuality

- Increased acceptance of infidelity and promiscuity.
- Increased likelihood of premarital sex, especially true for girls watching MTV and music videos.
- Increased likelihood of teen sexual activity by 3 to 6 times if watch TV apart from family.
- Decreased satisfaction with partner.

Sources:
Carroll, Jason S., et al, "Generation XXX: Pornography Acceptance and Use Among Emerging Adults," Journal of Adolescent Research, 2008, see Table 3.
Collins, Rebecca L., et al, "Watching Sex on Television Predicts Adolescent Initiation of Sexual Behavior," Pediatrics, 2004.
Strouse, J.S., "Gender and family as moderators of the relationship between music video exposure and adolescent sexual permissiveness," Adolescence, 1995.
Peterson, J.L., et al, "Television viewing and early initiation of sexual intercourse: Is there a link?," Journal of Homosexuality, 1991.
Zillmann, D. and Bryant, J. "Pornography's impact on sexual satisfaction," Journal of Applied Social Psychology, 1988.

Lasting Consequences of Media Sexuality

- Approximately 75% of all 18-19 years have had sexual intercourse.
- Only 11% of women married between 1990-1995 were virgins.
- Virginity at marriage decreases the likelihood of divorce by ¼ to ⅓.
- Approximately ⅔ of youth will cohabitate before marriage.
- Cohabitation almost doubles the likelihood of divorce.

Sources:
"Teenagers in the United States: Sexual Activity, Contraception Use and Childbearing, 2002," U.S. Department of Health and Human Services, December 2004, Figure 2.
"Fertility, Family Planning, and Women's Health: New Data from the 1995 National Survey of Family Growth," U.S. Department of Health and Human Services, Series 23, No. 19, May 1997, Table 25.
"The Social Organization of Sexuality - Sexual Practices in the United States," Laumann, Edward O., Gagnon, John H., Michael, Robert T. and Michaels, Stuart, University of Chicago Press, Table 5.8.
"The Social Organization of Sexuality - Sexual Practices in the United States," Laumann, Edward O., Gagnon, John H., Michael, Robert T. and Michaels, Stuart, University of Chicago Press, 1993, Figure 13.6

The issue is failed male leadership.

All of society is suffering from its consequences.

Small Group Discussion

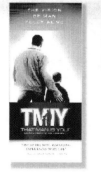

Starter Questions
1. How do you see greater societal events in the light of men's leadership responsibility?
2. How will you get control of the media in your household?
3. Please complete the survey's.

Next Week
The Four Leadership Roles of Men

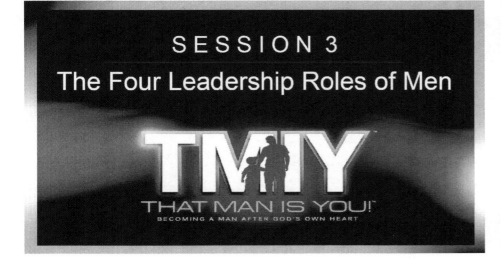

SESSION 3

The Four Leadership Roles of Men

TMY
THAT MAN IS YOU!™
BECOMING A MAN AFTER GOD'S OWN HEART

✝ The story of King David illustrates the consequences of failed male leadership. ✝

The Consequences for King David

1. Disharmony in the Family
"I will take your wives while you live to see it" (2 Samuel 12:11).

2. Children will Suffer
"The child that is born to you shall die" (2 Samuel 12:14).

3. Conflict in Society
"The sword shall not depart from your house" (2 Samuel 12:10).

4. Worship of God will Suffer
"David may not build a house for my name for he is a man of war and has shed blood" (1 Chronicles 22:8).

✝ By considering these four consequences in light of God's original blessing to humanity, we discover the four leadership roles entrusted to men. ✝

> And God blessed them saying, 'Increase and multiply and fill the earth and subdue it. And have dominion over the fishes of the sea and the fowls of the air and all the creatures that move upon the earth.
>
> Genesis 1:28

The Four Leadership Roles of Men

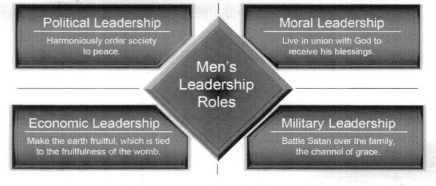

Men's Leadership Roles

Political Leadership
Harmoniously order society to peace.

Moral Leadership
Live in union with God to receive his blessings.

Economic Leadership
Make the earth fruitful, which is tied to the fruitfulness of the womb.

Military Leadership
Battle Satan over the family, the channel of grace.

The Hierarchy of Leadership Roles

Political Leadership

Economic Leadership

Military Leadership

Moral Leadership

The Breakdown of Male Leadership

Men's Leadership Roles

Political Leadership
Conflict is sown throughout greater society.

Moral Leadership
Separation from God.

Economic Leadership
The earth is barren, which is tied to the suffering of children.

Military Leadership
Satan sows disharmony in the home.

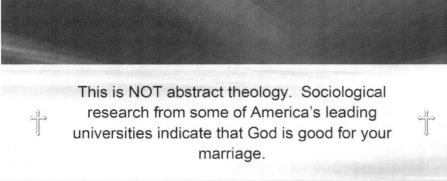

This is NOT abstract theology. Sociological research from some of America's leading universities indicate that God is good for your marriage.

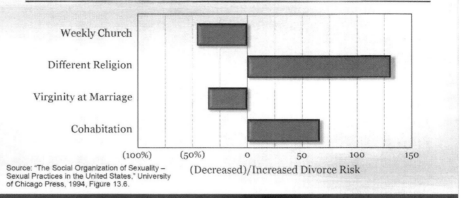

The Relationship between God and Marriage

Weekly Church

Different Religion

Virginity at Marriage

Cohabitation

(100%)   (50%)   0   50   100   150

(Decreased)/Increased Divorce Risk

Source: "The Social Organization of Sexuality – Sexual Practices in the United States," University of Chicago Press, 1994, Figure 13.6.

Further, research indicates that marriage makes you fruitful. It certainly leads to children. But it also leads to greater economic fruitfulness.

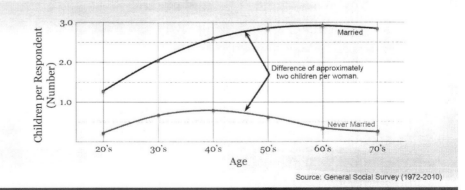

Marriage and Physical Fruitfulness

Children per Respondent (Number)

3.0

2.0

1.0

Married

Difference of approximately two children per woman.

Never Married

20's   30's   40's   50's   60's   70's

Age

Source: General Social Survey (1972-2010)

Leadership and Economic Fruitfulness

- Married men earn 30% more than unmarried men.
- Married households earn 12.4% more than a single man/woman combined.
- Divorce lowers immune system function.
- Divorce has same effect on heath as smoking one pack of cigarettes per day.
- Married men live 10 years longer than unmarried men.
- Being unmarried for a woman effects life expectancy similar to having cancer.

Source: Waite, Linda J. and Gallagher, Maggie, "The Case for Marriage – Why Married People are Happier, Healthier and Better Off Financially," Doubleday, 2000.

Marriage and Economic Fruitfulness

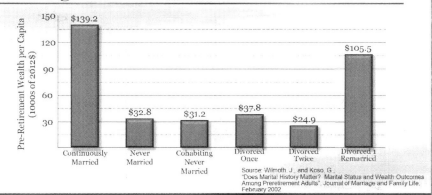

Source: Wilmoth, J., and Koso, G.,
"Does Marital History Matter? Marital Status and Wealth Outcomes Among Preretirement Adults", Journal of Marriage and Family Life, February 2002

Economic Fruitfulness into the Future

- Divorce doubles the likelihood a child will drop out of high school.
- Divorce reduces the likelihood of a child receiving a college degree by 1/3.
- College graduates earn on average twice as much as high school graduates.
- Children of divorce are 50% more likely to have health problems.
- Divorce reduces life expectancy of children by 4 years.

Source: Waite, Linda J. and Gallagher, Maggie, "The Case for Marriage – Why Married People are Happier, Healthier and Better Off Financially," Doubleday, 2000.

Marriage is good for your pocketbook. It is good for your personal peace and happiness and for that of your children.

Marriage and Peace and Happiness

- Married couples are 60% more likely to be happy with their lives.
- Married couples have more frequent sex.
- Church going spouses are 22% more likely to be sexually satisfied than non-church going spouses.
- Divorce significantly increases depression and triples the likelihood a person will commit suicide.
- Divorced people are 2.5X more likely than married persons to be unhappy with their lives.

Source: Waite, Linda J. and Gallagher, Maggie, "The Case for Marriage – Why Married People are Happier, Healthier and Better Off Financially," Doubleday, 2000.

Peace and Happiness into the Future

- Single and divorced women are almost ten times more likely to be raped than wives.
- Cohabitation significantly increases the likelihood of a woman being raped or physically assaulted.
- Divorce doubles the likelihood of sexual intercourse by age 14 and triples the likelihood of becoming an unwed mother.
- Divorce doubles the likelihood that a child will be incarcerated for a crime.
- Divorce increases the likelihood of mental illness in a child by 37%.

Source: Waite, Linda J. and Gallagher, Maggie, "The Case for Marriage – Why Married People are Happier, Healthier and Better Off Financially," Doubleday, 2000.

It's really quite simple. God created the union of man and woman to be the channel by which he blesses the world. It remains true to this day.

Small Group Discussion

Starter Questions
1. How will you live in greater union with God so that you can receive his blessings?
2. What can you do to strengthen families – your own and others?

Next Week
The Five Traits of Authentic Leaders

SESSION 4
The Five Traits of Authentic Leaders

TMIY
THAT MAN IS YOU!
BECOMING A MAN AFTER GOD'S OWN HEART

The Four Leadership Roles of Men

Political Leadership
Harmoniously order society to peace.

Moral Leadership
Live in union with God to receive his blessings.

Men's Leadership Roles

Economic Leadership
Make the earth fruitful, which is tied to the fruitfulness of the womb.

Military Leadership
Battle Satan over the family, the channel of grace.

And God blessed them saying, 'Increase and multiply and fill the earth and subdue it. And have dominion over the fishes of the sea and the fowls of the air and all the creatures that move upon the earth.

Genesis 1:28

The Hierarchy of Leadership Roles

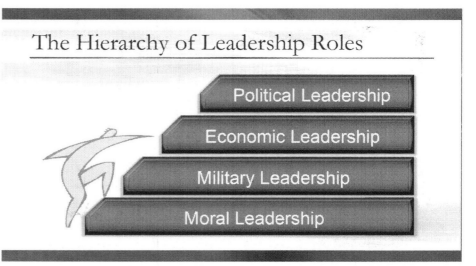

Political Leadership

Economic Leadership

Military Leadership

Moral Leadership

To fulfill the four leadership roles with which you have been entrusted, you must develop within yourself the five traits of authentic leaders.

The Five Traits of Authentic Leaders

Foundation for Future
Lays a foundation for the future in the midst of actions today.

Personal Responsibility
The willingness to take personal responsibility for actions.

Sacrifice
The willingness to pay the price.

Integrity of Action
The discipline to ensure all actions are consistent with mission.

Clarity of Thought
The ability to maintain clarity of thought in all decisions.

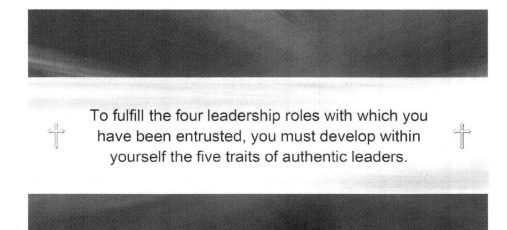

Fulfilling Authentic Male Leadership

Political Leadership
Foundation for Future

Moral Leadership
Personal Responsibility

Sacrifice
The willingness to pay the price.

Economic Leadership
Foundation for Future

Military Leadership
Clarity of Thought
Integrity of Action

King David combined a failure in moral leadership with an unwillingness to take personal responsibility for his actions. All Israel paid the price.

David said to the messenger, '... Do not let this matter trouble you, for the sword devours now one and now another' ... But the thing that David had done displeased the Lord. And the Lord sent Nathan to him, and said to him ... 'I will take your wives before your eyes ... you did it secretly; but I will do this thing before all Israel.'

2 Samuel 11:25-12:12

Men have struggled with a willingness to take personal responsibility for their actions from the beginning.

The Lord God took the man and put him in the garden of Eden to till it and keep it. And the Lord God commanded the man, saying, 'You may freely eat of every tree of the garden, but of the tree of the knowledge of good and evil you shall not eat, for in the day that you eat of it you shall die.

Genesis 2:15-17

The serpent was more subtle than any other wild creature that the Lord God had made. He said to the woman, 'Did God say, `You shall not eat of any tree of the garden?` ... You will not die. For God knows that when you eat of it your eyes will be opened, and you will be like God, knowing good and evil.'

Genesis 3:1-5

When the woman saw that the tree was good for food, and that it was a delight to the eyes, and that the tree was to be desired to make one wise, she took of its fruit and ate; and she also gave some to her husband, and he ate.

Genesis 3:6

And the eyes of them both were opened: and when they perceived themselves to be naked, they sewed together fig leaves, and made themselves clothes. And when they heard the voice of the Lord God walking in paradise at the afternoon air, Adam and his wife hid themselves from the face of the Lord God amidst the trees of paradise.

Genesis 3:7-8

But the Lord God called to the man, and said to him, 'Where are you? ... Who told you that you were naked? Have you eaten of the tree of which I commanded you not to eat?' The man said, 'The woman whom thou gavest me to be with me, she gave me fruit of the tree, and I ate.'

Genesis 3:9-12

I will greatly multiply your pain in childbearing; in pain you shall bring forth children, yet your desire shall be for your husband, and he shall rule over you.

Genesis 3:16

> Cursed is the ground because of you; in toil you shall eat of it all the days of your life; thorns and thistles it shall bring forth to you … In the sweat of your face you shall eat bread till you return to the ground for out of it your were taken; you are dust and to dust you shall return.
>
> Genesis 3:17-19

The Breakdown in Adam's Leadership

Political Leadership
"Your desire shall be for your husband, and he shall rule over you."

Moral Leadership
Disobeys God and then hides from God.

Men's Leadership Roles

Economic Leadership
"Thorns and thistles it shall bring forth to you."

Military Leadership
Allows Satan to approach Eve.

The issue of male leadership is NOT first and foremost about us. Our actions have ramifications that impact all of society.

Small Group Discussion

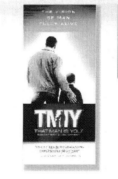

Starter Questions

1. When was the most difficult time that you stepped up to take responsibility for your actions?
2. How can you prepare yourself to take responsibility for your actions in difficult situations?

Next Week
Steadfast Leadership

SESSION 5
Steadfast Leadership

TMIY
THAT MAN IS YOU!
BECOMING A MAN AFTER GOD'S OWN HEART

Fulfilling Authentic Male Leadership

| Political Leadership
Foundation for Future | | Moral Leadership
Personal Responsibility |
|---|---|---|
| | **Sacrifice**
The willingness to
pay the price. | |
| Economic Leadership
Foundation for Future | | Military Leadership
Clarity of Thought
Integrity of Action |

To become an authentic leader, you must maintain clarity of thought and integrity of action.

The Story of King Solomon

- Born approximately 1000 B.C.
- Second son born to King David and Bathsheba.
- Through the intercession of Bathsheba, King David appoints him as successor.
- Reigns 40 years (971 – 931 B.C.).
- Israel experiences great peace, prosperity and influence.

I am about to go the way of all the earth. Be strong, and show yourself a man, and keep the charge of the Lord your God, walking in his ways and keeping his statutes ... that the Lord may establish his word which he spoke concerning me, saying, 'If your sons take heed to their way, to walk before me in faithfulness with all their heart and with all their soul, there shall not fail you a man on the throne of Israel.'

1 Kings 2:1-4

The Lord appeared to Solomon in a dream by night; and God said, 'Ask what I shall give you.' And Solomon said, '... Give thy servant therefore an understanding mind to govern thy people, that I may discern between good and evil' ... And God said to him, '... I now do according to your word. Behold, I give you a wise and discerning mind ... I give you also what you have not asked , both riches and honor.

1 Kings 3:5-14

King Solomon and all the congregation of Israel [were] sacrificing so many sheep and oxen that they could not be counted or numbered ... a cloud filled the house of the Lord ... for the glory of the Lord filled the house of the Lord. Then Solomon said, '... O Lord, God of Israel, there is no God like thee ... Let your heart therefore be wholly true to the Lord our God, walking in his statutes and keeping his commandments.'

1 Kings 8:1-61

I have acquired great wisdom, surpassing all who were over Jerusalem before me ... I perceived that this also is but a striving after wind ... I searched with my mind how to cheer my body with wine ... I made great works ... whatever my eyes desired I did not keep from them; I kept my heart from no pleasure ... and behold all was vanity and a striving after wind ... so I hated life ... and gave my heart up to despair.

Ecclesiastes 1:16 – 2:20

Now King Solomon loved many foreign women … Solomon clung to these in love … and when Solomon was old his wives turned away his heart after other gods; and his heart was not wholly true to the Lord his God, as was the heart of David his father. For Solomon went after Ashtoreth the goddess of the Sidonians, and after Milcom the abomination of the Ammonites. So Solomon did what was evil in the sight of the Lord.

1 Kings 11:1-8

And the Lord was angry with Solomon, because his heart had turned away from the Lord, the God of Israel, who had appeared to him twice, and had commanded him concerning this thing … Therefore the Lord said to Solomon, 'since this has been your mind … I will surely tear the kingdom from you and will give it to your servant. Yet for the sake of David your father I will not do it in your days, but I will tear it out of the hand of your son.'

1 Kings 11:9-13

Saints can become great leaders because they remain steadfastly united to God.

Mother Teresa of Calcutta

- 1910: Born August 26th in Albania.
- 1918: Death of Father.
- 1928: Joins Sister of Loreto in Ireland.
- 1929: Arrives in India.
- 1946: Inspiration on September 10th.
- 1948: Enters slums on August 17th.
- 1950: Founds Missionaries of Charity.
- 1979: Wins Noble Peace Prize.
- 1997: Dies on September 5th.
- 2003: Beatified on October 20th.

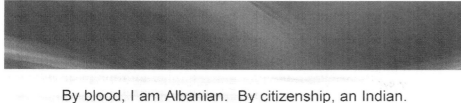

"By blood, I am Albanian. By citizenship, an Indian. By faith, I am a Catholic nun. As to my calling, I belong to the world. As to my heart, I belong entirely to the Heart of Jesus."

Mother Teresa

"You have become my Spouse for my love – you have come to India for Me. The thirst you had for souls brought you so far. Are you afraid to take one more step for your Spouse – for Me – for souls? Is your generosity grown cold – am I a second to you?"

Jesus to Mother Teresa

"For me it is so clear – everything in the Missionaries of Charity exists only to satiate Jesus. His words on the wall of every Missionaries of Charity chapel, they are not from [the] past only, but alive here and now, spoken to you."

Jesus to Mother Teresa

Clarity of Thought for Mother Teresa

- "Truly, I say to you, as you did it to one of the least of my brethren, you did it to me" (Matthew 25:40).
- "They are Jesus. Each one is Jesus in a distressing disguise" (Mother Teresa).

Integrity of Action for Mother Teresa

- "To bring souls to God – and God to souls."
- "To be Indian – to live with them – like them – so as to get at the people's heart."
- Perfect poverty: Own absolutely nothing. Even the clothes are kept in common.
- Live in poverty: No carpeting. No hot water. No servants. Perform own housework.
- Eat with the poor they serve.

" We are not social workers. We may be doing social work in the eyes of some people, but we must be contemplatives in the heart of the world. "

Mother Teresa

The issue is the adoration of God. With Mother Teresa, we must learn to find and adore him in the midst of the world.

Small Group Discussion

Starter Questions
1. When have you lost focus and what were the consequences?
2. How do you make sure that all your actions help you fulfill your fundamental purpose?

Next Week
Attaining Clarity of Thought

SESSION 6
Attaining Clarity of Thought

Fulfilling Authentic Male Leadership

Political Leadership Foundation for Future	Moral Leadership Personal Responsibility

Sacrifice
The willingness to pay the price.

Economic Leadership Foundation for Future	Military Leadership Clarity of Thought Integrity of Action

Mother Teresa maintained clarity of thought and integrity of action so profoundly that she became a saint AND she established an order that continues to transform millions of lives around the world.

Clarity of Thought for Mother Teresa

- "Truly, I say to you, as you did it to one of the least of my brethren, you did it to me" (Matthew 25:40).

- "They are Jesus. Each one is Jesus in a distressing disguise" (Mother Teresa).

The Clarifying Principle

- Easily grasped and enunciated.
- Organizes thoughts by coherently explaining external reality.
- Organizes actions by providing focal point to a diversity of actions.
- Defines principles.

The Clarifying Principle

God is found in communion.

The Lord God formed man of dust from the ground, and breathed into his nostrils the breath of life: and man became a living being. And the Lord God planted a garden in Eden, in the east; and there he put the man whom he had formed. And out of the ground the Lord God made to grow every tree that is pleasant to the sight and good for food.

Genesis 2:7-9

The Lord God took the man and put him in the garden of Eden to till it and keep it ... Then the Lord God said, 'It is not good that the man should be alone; I will make a helper fit for him.'

Genesis 2:15-18

So out of the ground the Lord God formed every beast of the field and every bird of the air, and brought them to the man to see what he would call them; and whatever the man called every living creature, that was its name … but for the man there was not found a helper fit for him.

Genesis 2:19-20

So the Lord God caused a deep sleep to fall upon the man, and while he slept took one of his ribs and closed up its place with flesh; and the rib with the Lord God had taken from the man he made into a woman and brought her to the man.

Genesis 2:21-22

Then the man said, 'This at last is bone of my bones and flesh of my flesh; she shall be called Woman, because she was take out of Man.' Therefore a man leaves his father and his mother and cleaves to his wife, and they become one flesh. And the man and his wife were both naked, and were not ashamed.

Genesis 2:23-25

And God blessed them saying, 'Increase and multiply and fill the earth and subdue it. And have dominion over the fishes of the sea and the fowls of the air and all the creatures that move upon the earth.

Genesis 1:28

God gives the blessing to the union of man and woman because God dwells in the union of man and woman.

God's Presence in the Spousal Union

- "Where two or three are gathered in my name, there am I in the midst of them" (Matthew 18:20).

- "Shelly receive this ring as a sign of my love and fidelity. In the name of the Father, and of the Son and of the Holy Spirit" (Marriage Ceremony).

To receive a blessing from God is to have an encounter with God.

The Blessing of Fruitfulness

- "And God blessed them, and God said to them, 'Be fruitful and multiply and fill the earth and subdue it" (Genesis 1:28).

- "Therefore the Lord himself will give you a sign. Behold, a virgin [maiden] shall conceive and bear a son, and shall call his name Emmanuel [which means God is with us]" (Isaiah 7:14).

God's Presence in the Child

- "Whoever receives one such child in my name receives me" (Matthew 18:5).
- "By His incarnation the Son of God has united Himself in some fashion with every man" (Second Vatican Council, *Gaudium et Spes*, #22).

God's promises to dwell in the midst of the spousal union and in our children are as profound as the one he made to transform Mother Teresa into a saint.

Integrity of Action for Mother Teresa

We are not social workers. We may be doing social work in the eyes of some people, but we must be contemplatives in the heart of the world.

Mother Teresa

To contemplate the face of Christ, and to contemplate it with Mary, is the 'programme' which I have set before the Church at the dawn of the third millennium, summoning her to put out into the deep on the sea of history with the enthusiasm of the new evangelization.

Pope John Paul II
Ecclesia de Eucaristia, #6

The Christian family constitutes a specific revelation and realization of ecclesial communion, and for this reason it can and should be called a domestic church.

Pope John Paul II
Familiaris Consortio, #21

We have attained clarity of thought: God is found in communion. He is dwelling in our midst. We must have the integrity of action to glimpse his hidden face.

Small Group Discussion

Starter Questions
1. In what ways do you find God dwelling in the midst of your marriage and family life?
2. In what ways do you manifest Christ to your wife and children?

Next Week
Developing Integrity of Action

SESSION 7
Developing Integrity of Action

TMIY™
THAT MAN IS YOU!™
BECOMING A MAN AFTER GOD'S OWN HEART

Fulfilling Authentic Male Leadership

Political Leadership Foundation for Future	Moral Leadership Personal Responsibility

Sacrifice
The willingness to pay the price.

Economic Leadership Foundation for Future	Military Leadership Clarity of Thought Integrity of Action

The pathway to authentic leadership is found in maintaining clarity of thought and integrity of action while remaining united to God.

The Path of Mother Teresa

- "Truly, I say to you, as you did it to one of the least of my brethren, you did it for me" (Matthew 25:40).
- **Clarity of Thought:** "They are Jesus. Each one is Jesus in a distressing disguise."
- **Integrity of Action:** "We must be contemplatives in the midst of the world."

Clarity of Thought for Men

- God is found in communion.
- "Where two or three are gathered in my name, there am I in the midst of them" (Matthew 18:20).
- "Whoever receives one such child in my name receives me" (Matthew 18:5).

In our Nuptial Mass, the Church identified for us the pathway for developing integrity of action within the home.

Integrity of Action in the Home

Integrity of Action

Gift of Fatherhood
"Will you accept children loving from God and raise them according to the laws of Christ and his Church?"

Gift of Bridegroom
"Will you love and honor each other as man and wife for the rest of your lives?"

Self-Possession
"Have you come here freely and without reservation to give yourselves to each other in marriage?"

The fundamental issue is freedom. You must possess yourself in order to give yourself away.

The Enslavement of Sin

- "Have you come here freely and without reservation to give yourselves to each other in marriage?"
- "He who sins is the slave of sin" (John 8:34).
- "For all that is in the world, the lust of the flesh and the lust of the eyes and the pride of life, is not of the Father but is of the world" (1 John 2:16).

Freedom in Christ

- "If you continue in my word, you are truly my disciples, and you will know the truth, and the truth will make you free" (John 8:31-32)
- "Show yourself a man, and keep the charge of the Lord your God, walking in his ways and keeping his statutes" (1 Kings 2:2-3).
- You must bind yourself to Christ.

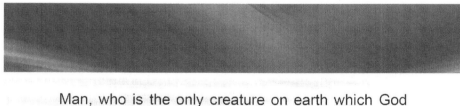

Man, who is the only creature on earth which God willed for itself, cannot fully find himself except through a sincere gift of himself.

Second Vatican Council
Gaudium et Spes, #24

The Challenge of Christian Marriage

- "Will you love and honor each other as man and wife for the rest of your lives?"
- "What therefore God has joined together, let no man put asunder" (Matthew 19:6).
- "If such is the case of a man with his wife, it is not expedient to marry" (Matthew 19:10).

> Every one then who hears these words of mine and does them will be like a wise man who built his house upon the rock; and the rain fell, and the floods came, and the winds blew and beat upon that house, but it did not fall, because it had been founded on the rock.
>
> Matthew 7:24-27

Jesus Christ: the Foundation of Marriage

- "Where two or three are gathered in my name, there am I in the midst of them" (Matthew 16:20).
- "Shelly, receive this ring as a sign of my love and fidelity. In the name of the Father. And of the Son. And of the Holy Spirit. Amen."
- You must bind your marriage to Jesus Christ.

Together, bridegroom and bride are called to offer their union to God so that they may receive the blessing of God.

The Mystery of the Child

- "Will you accept children lovingly from God and raise them according to the laws of Christ and his Church?"
- "Whoever receives one such child in my name receives me" (Matthew 18:5).
- "For by His incarnation the Son of God has united Himself in some fashion with every man" (*Gaudium et Spes*, #22).

The Hidden Life of Christ

- "It is no longer I who live, but Christ who lives in me" (Galatians 2:20).
- "Some belong to the bodily and spiritual life simultaneously, which takes place in the sacrament of matrimony where a man and woman come together to beget offspring and to rear them in divine worship" (St. Thomas Aquinas).
- You must unite your children to Christ so that they may attain to the full stature of Christ.

Integrity of action simply involves uniting ourselves and those entrusted to us to Christ.

Integrity of Action

- We must unite ourselves to Christ so that we may gain possession of ourselves.
- We must unite our marriages to Christ so that they can withstand the storms of time.
- We must unite our children to Christ so that they may attain to the full stature of Christ.

Small Group Discussion

Starter Questions

1. In what ways do you need to gain better possession of yourself?
2. How can you more surely unite your marriages and children to Christ?

Next Week
Laying a Foundation for the Future

Clarity of Thought for Men

- God is found in communion.
- "Where two or three are gathered in my name, there am I in the midst of them" (Matthew 18:20).
- "Whoever receives one such child in my name receives me" (Matthew 18:5).

Integrity of Action

- We must unite ourselves to Christ so that we may gain possession of ourselves.
- We must unite our marriages to Christ so that they can withstand the storms of time.
- We must unite our children to Christ so that they may attain to the full stature of Christ.

Authentic male leadership is called to be selfless versus selfish.

King Henry VIII

- 1485: Henry VII usurps throne of England.
- 1491: Henry VIII is born.
- 1509: Marries Catherine of Aragon; Crowned King of England.
- 1533: Marries Anne Boleyn
- 1534: Declared Head of Church in England.
- 1536: Executes Anne Boleyn
- 1536-1547: Marries 4 additional wives.
- 1547: Dies on January 8th.

King Henry VIII: Economic Straits

- 1509: Inherits England in sound financial condition.
- 1509ff: Lives as a man of excess.
- 1511: Enters conflict with France.
- 1534: Declared "Head of Church."
- 1536-1538: Dissolution of monasteries.
- 1540ff: Dissipates money from the dissolution of monasteries.
- 1544: Borrows money to invade France.

King Henry VIII: Political Chaos

- 1547: Henry VIII dies; Edward VI (from Jane Seymour) becomes king at age 9. Council deepens divide with Catholicism.
- 1553: Edward VI dies; Mary I (from Catherine of Aragon) becomes queen; re-establishes Catholicism.
- 1558: Mary dies; Elizabeth I (from Anne Boleyn) becomes queen; returns to Protestantism.
- 1603: Elizabeth dies.
- Henry had 1 son; 2 daughters; 1 illegitimate son; 2 illegitimate daughters (?).
- No grandchildren; House of Tudor ends.

King Henry VIII's failure in Moral Leadership resulted in the four consequences of failed male leadership being poured out upon England.

Gary S. Becker

- Born in Pennsylvania in 1930.
- Received Bachelor from Princeton.
- Received PhD from University of Chicago.
- Taught at Columbia and Chicago.
- Held joint chair in Economics and Sociology.
- Studied human capital and the family.
- Received Nobel Laureate in Economics in 1992.
- Praised by Vatican.

Human Capital and Economic Growth

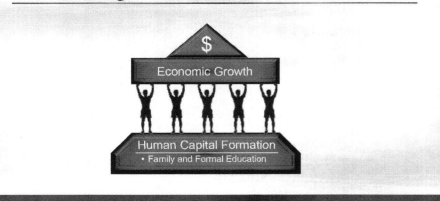

The Family and Human Capital

Reduced Social Costs
- Reduced physical and mental health issues.
- Reduced crime.
- Reduced sexual activity.

Spousal Specialization
- Provides for needs today.
- Provides formation for tomorrow.

Enhanced Earnings
- Greater Educational attainment.
- Increased earnings.
- More stable marriages.

The Family Dinner and Self-Esteem

- Comparing teens who eat dinner with family at least 5 nights per week versus those who do so only 2 nights per week.
- Teens are nearly one and half times more likely to say that their parents are proud of them.
- Teens are forty percent more likely to confide in their parents with a serious problem.
- Parents are half as likely to say that they do not know their children's friends very well.

Sources:
The National Center on Addiction and Substance Abuse at Columbia University (CASA). "The Importance of Family Dinners II," September, 2005.
The National Center on Addiction and Substance Abuse at Columbia University (CASA). "The Importance of Family Dinners III," September, 2006.

The Reality of Peer Pressure

- Peer pressure strongly influences sexual activity and substance abuse.
- Almost 80 percent of college students were introduced to alcohol by their friends.
- Almost 95 percent of college students were introduced to drugs by their friends.
- Drinking in college is correlated to the number of offers a student receives to drink.

Sources:
The National Center on Addiction and Substance Abuse at Columbia University (CASA). National Survey of American Attitudes on Substance Abuse X: Teens and Parents, August, 2005.
The National Center on Addiction and Substance Abuse at Columbia University (CASA). "Wasting the Best and Brightest: Substance e Abuse at America's Colleges and Universities. 2007. pp. 53 -54.

The Family and Education

- Teens who eat dinner with their families at least 5 nights per week are almost twice as likely to get A's as those who eat dinner with their families 2 or less nights per week.
- Divorce doubles the likelihood that a child will drop out of High School.
- Divorce reduces the likelihood of a child receiving a college degree by approximately ⅓.

Sources:
The National Center on Addiction and Substance Abuse at Columbia University (CASA). "The Importance of Family Dinners," September, 2003.
Waite, Linda J and Gallagher, Maggie. "The Case for Marriage." Doubleday, 2000.

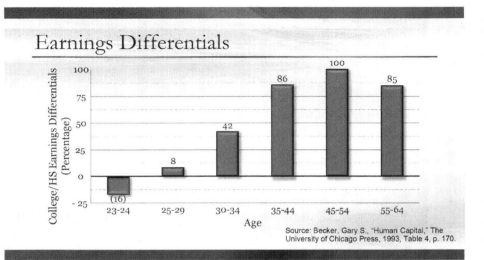

Earnings Differentials

Source: Becker, Gary S., "Human Capital," The University of Chicago Press, 1993, Table 4, p. 170.

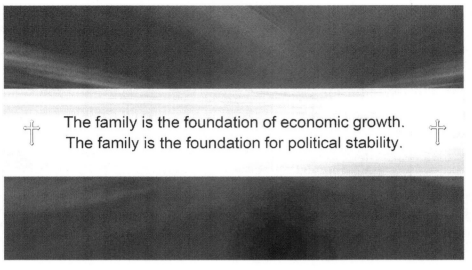

The family is the foundation of economic growth.
The family is the foundation for political stability.

The natural family, as an intimate communion of life and love, based on marriage between a man and a woman, constitutes 'the primary place of `humanization` for the person and society' … For this reason, the family is the first and indispensable teacher of peace.

Pope Benedict XVI
World Day of Peace, 2008

The Family and Peace

- Divorce doubles the likelihood of experimentation with illegal substances.
- Divorce increases the likelihood of mental illnesses in a child by 37 percent.
- Divorce doubles the likelihood that a child will be incarcerated for a crime.
- Divorce doubles the likelihood that a child will begin having sex by age 14.
- Divorce triples the likelihood that a girl will be an unwed mother.

Source:
Waite, Linda J. and Gallagher, Maggie. "The Case for Marriage," Doubleday, 2000.

A Sustainable Socioeconomic Model

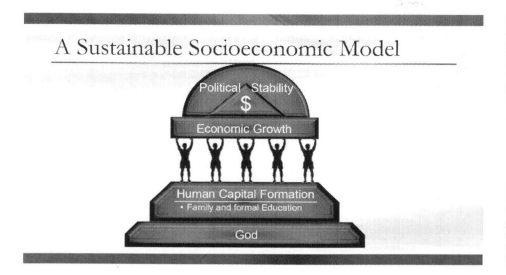

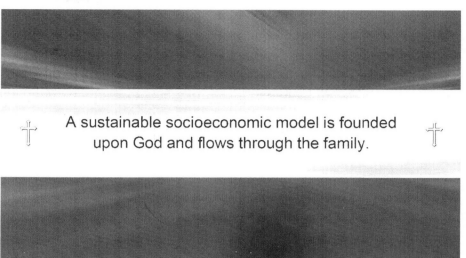

A sustainable socioeconomic model is founded upon God and flows through the family.

Small Group Discussion

Starter Questions
1. How are you forming your children to be the foundation for the future?
2. How are your actions consistent or inconsistent with the proper formation of your children?

Next Week
The Willingness to Pay the Price

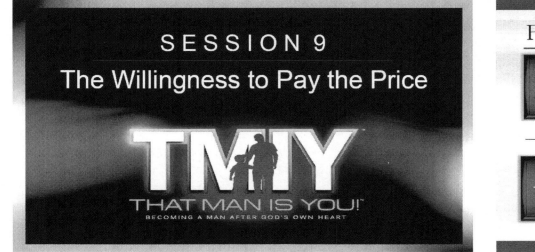

SESSION 9
The Willingness to Pay the Price

Fulfilling Authentic Male Leadership

Political Leadership	Moral Leadership
Foundation for Future	Personal Responsibility

Sacrifice
The willingness to pay the price.

Economic Leadership	Military Leadership
Foundation for Future	Clarity of Thought Integrity of Action

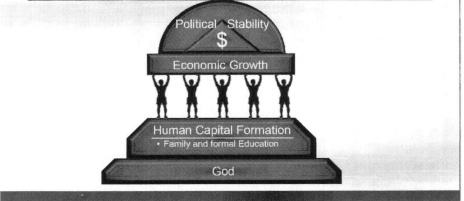

A Sustainable Socioeconomic Model

Political Stability
$
Economic Growth
Human Capital Formation
• Family and formal Education
God

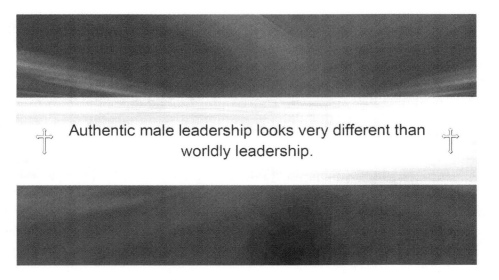

Authentic male leadership looks very different than worldly leadership.

The Kingship of Jesus Christ

1. Jesus Christ is the "new Adam"
"For as in Adam all die, so also in Christ shall all be made alive" (1 Corinthians 15:22).

2. Jesus Christ is the "son of David"
"Jesus, Son of David, have mercy on me" (Luke 18:38).

3. Jesus Christ as the "king of the Jews"
"Pilate wrote a title and put it on the cross, Jesus of Nazareth, the King of the Jews" (John 19:19).

4. Jesus Christ is the "head of the Church"
"Jesus Christ is the head of the Church" (Ephesians 5:23).

The Humble Beginnings of Christ

- "While they were there, the time came for her to be delivered. And she gave birth to her first-born son and wrapped him in swaddling cloths, and laid him in a manger, because there was no place for them in the inn" (Luke 2:6-7).

- "They brought Jesus up to Jerusalem to present him to the Lord … to offer sacrifice … a pair of turtledoves, or two young pigeons" (Luke 2:22-24).

The Obscure Youth of Christ

- "Rise, take the child and his mother, and go to the land of Israel … Joseph rose and took the child and his mother, … and dwelt in … Nazareth" (Matthew 2:20-23).

- "Nathanael said to Philip, 'Can anything good come out of Nazareth?'" (John 1:46).

- "Where did this man get this wisdom and these mighty works? Is not this the carpenter's son?" … And they took offense at him" (Matthew 13:54-57).

An Ignominious Death for Christ

- "You will all fall away; for it is written, 'I will strike the shepherd, and the sheep will be scattered'" (Mark 14:27).

- "Away with him, away with him, crucify him" (John 19:15).

- "Then two robbers were crucified with him, one on the right and one on the left" (Matthew 27:38).

- "Because … the tomb was close at hand, they laid Jesus there" (John 19:42).

As God, Christ manifests for us in its entirety the mystery of authentic leadership.

The Moral Leadership of Christ

- Live in union with God.
- "I and the Father are one" (John 10:30).
- "Have I been with you so long, and yet you do not know me, Philip? He who has seen me has seen the Father … The words that I say to you I do not speak on my own authority; but the Father who dwells in me does his works" (John 14:9-11).

The Military Leadership of Christ

- Battle Satan over the family.
- "Begone, Satan! for it is written, 'You shall worship the Lord you God and him only shall you serve'" (Matthew 3:10).
- "Husbands, love your wives, as Christ loved the church and gave himself up for her … that he might present the church to himself in splendor, without spot or wrinkle or any such thing" (Ephesians 5:25-27).

The Economic Leadership of Christ

- Make the earth fruitful.
- "Taking the five loaves and two fish Jesus looked up to heaven, and blessed, and broke and gave the loaves to the disciples, and the disciples gave them to the crowds … and they took up twelve baskets [of fragments]. And those who ate were about five thousand men, besides women and children" (Matthew 14:13-21).

The Political Leadership of Christ

- Harmoniously order society to peace.
- "Peace I leave with you; my peace I give to you; not as the world gives do I give to you" (John 14:27).
- "Jesus came and stood among them and said to them, 'Peace be with you' … Jesus said to them again, 'Peace be with you … Receive the Holy Spirit.'" (John 20:19-23).

As God, Christ perfectly possesses the five traits of authentic leaders.

The Ultimate Teaching of Christ

1. "Father, forgive them; for they know not what they do" (Luke 23:34).
2. "Today, you will be with me in Paradise" (Luke 23:43).
3. "Woman, behold your son … Disciple, behold your mother" (John 19:26-27).
4. "My God, my God, why have you forsaken me" (Matthew 27:46)?
5. "I thirst" (John 19:28).
6. "It is consummated" (John 19:30).
7. "Into your hands I commend my spirit" (Luke 23:46).

The Personal Responsibility of Christ

- "Father, forgive them; for they know not what they do" (Luke 23:34).
- "He was despised and rejected by men; a man of sorrows, and acquainted with grief … Surely he has borne our griefs and carried our sorrows … he was wounded for our transgressions, he was bruised for our iniquities; upon him was the chastisement that made us whole, and with his stripes we are healed" (Isaiah 53:3-5).

Clarity of Thought for Christ

- "Today, you will be with me in Paradise" (Luke 23:43).
- "I thirst" (John 19:28).
- "Father, the hour has come; glorify thy Son that the Son may glorify thee ... this is eternal life, that they know thee the only true God, and Jesus Christ whom thou hast sent. I glorified thee on earth, having accomplished the work which thou gavest me to do ... now I am no more in the world ... and I am coming to thee" (John 17:1-11).

Integrity of Action for Christ

- "I will no longer talk much with you, for the ruler of this world is coming. He has no power over me; but I do as the Father has commanded me, so that the world may know that I love the Father" (John 14:30-31).
- "It is consummated" (John 19:30).
- "Into your hands I commend my spirit" (Luke 23:46).

Christ's Foundation for the Future

- "Woman, behold your son ... Disciple, behold your mother" (John 19:26-27).
- "When the time had fully come, God sent forth his Son, born of woman, born under the law, to redeem those who were under the law, so that we might receive adoption as sons. And because you are sons, God has sent his Spirit of his Son into our hearts, crying, 'Abba! Father!'" (Galatians 4:4-6).

Christ's Willingness to Pay the Price

- "My God, my God, why have you forsaken me" (Matthew 27:46)?
- "Though he was in the form of God, [Jesus Christ] did not count equality with God a thing to be grasped, but emptied himself, taking the form of a servant, being born in the likeness of men. And being found in human form he humbled himself and became obedient unto death, even death on a cross" (Philippians 2:6-7).

The fruitfulness of Christ's leadership is so superabundant that the entire world is blessed in Jesus Christt.

Therefore God has highly exalted him and bestowed on him the name which is above every name, that at the name of Jesus every knee should bow, heaven and on earth and under the earth, and every tongue confess that Jesus Christ is Lord, to the glory of God the Father.

Philippians 2:9-11

Small Group Discussion

Starter Questions

1. When did you choose the wrong path because you were unwilling to pay the price? What did you learn?
2. When did you pay the price to fulfill God's will in your life?

Next Week
Authentic Leadership in the Home

SESSION 10

Authentic Leadership in the Home

TMIY

THAT MAN IS YOU!

BECOMING A MAN AFTER GOD'S OWN HEART

Fulfilling Authentic Male Leadership

Political Leadership
Foundation for Future

Moral Leadership
Personal Responsibility

Sacrifice
The willingness to
pay the price.

Economic Leadership
Foundation for Future

Military Leadership
Clarity of Thought
Integrity of Action

 St. Joseph lived his life as an authentic leader within the context of the Holy Family so well that he became the second greatest saint in heaven.

The Reality of the Holy Family

1. The Dignity of Christ
The greatest dignity belongs to Christ, who is the Word Incarnate.

2. The Dignity of the Mother of God
Mary has the second greatest dignity. She is the Mother of God and the Immaculate Conception.

3. The Dignity of St. Joseph
St. Joseph has the "lowest" dignity. He is the just man of Scripture and the second greatest saint in heaven.

St. Joseph as the Leader of the Holy Family

- "Joseph, son of David, do not fear to take Mary your wife" (Matthew 1:20ff).
- "And at the end of eight days, when he was circumcised, he was called Jesus, the name given by the angel" (Luke 2:21).
- "Rise, take the child and his mother, and flee into Egypt" (Matthew 2:13ff).
- "Rise, take the child and his mother, and go to the land of Israel" (Matthew 2:19ff).

The Leadership of St. Joseph

- Personal Responsibility: "Joseph, being a just man" (Matthew 1:19).
- Clarity of Thought: "Joseph, son of David, do not fear to take Mary your wife" (Matthew 1:20).
- Integrity of Action: "Joseph … took the child and his mother by night, and departed for Egypt (Matthew 2:14).
- Foundation for the Future: "Jesus was obedient to them" (Luke 2:51).
- Pay the Price: "Joseph resolved to send her away quietly" (Matthew 1:19).

St. Joseph's Gift as Bridegroom

- "Joseph, being a just man and unwilling to [expose her to the law], resolved to send her away quietly" (Matthew 1:19).
- "Husbands, love your wives, as Christ loved the Church and gave himself up for her … that she might be holy and without blemish" (Ephesians 5:25-27).
- "I desire mercy and not sacrifice" (Matthew 12:7).

St. Joseph's Gift as Father

- "[Jesus] went down with them and came to Nazareth, and was obedient to them" (Luke 2:51).
- "The admirable St. Joseph was given to the earth to express the adorable perfection of God the Father in a tangible way" (Fr. Andrew Doze).
- "Men relive and reveal on earth the very Fatherhood of God" (Pope John Paul II).

Integrity of Action in the Home

Integrity of Action

Gift of Fatherhood
"Will you accept children loving from God and raise them according to the laws of Christ and his Church?"

Gift of Bridegroom
"Will you love and honor each other as man and wife for the rest of your lives?"

Self-Possession
"Have you come here freely and without reservation to give yourselves to each other in marriage?"

Authentic Leadership in the Holy Family

- St. Joseph remains steadfastly united to God to fulfill his will.
- St. Joseph protects Mary and the spousal union.
- The leadership of St. Joseph helps Mary embrace the vulnerability of saying "yes" to God.
- The world is transformed through Jesus Christ.

The Selflessness of St. Joseph's Leadership

- "Learn of me, because I am meek and humble of heart" (Matthew 11:29).
- "The kings of the Gentiles exercise lordship over them; and those in authority over them are called benefactors. But not so with you; rather let the greatest among you become as the youngest, and the leader as one who serves" (Luke 22:25-26).

✝ The Holy Family provided a model of family life so profound that it was destined to change the world. ✝

The Roman Empire

- Dominate military and economic power in the world.
- Emperor and pagan god worship.
- Sexual immorality.
- Unstable family life characterized by a lack of children.
- A falling population.

Two Models of the Family

Ancient Rome	Christianity
• Unstable marriages.	• Consistent moral requirements.
• Refusal to enter marriage.	• Stable marriages.
• Below replacement fertility rate.	• High fertility rate.
• Contraception.	• No contraception.
• Abortion.	• No abortion.
• Infanticide.	• No infanticide.
• Decreasing population.	• Increasing population.

Source: Stark, Rodney, "The Rise of Christianity," HarperCollins, 1997.

The Changing Reality of Rome

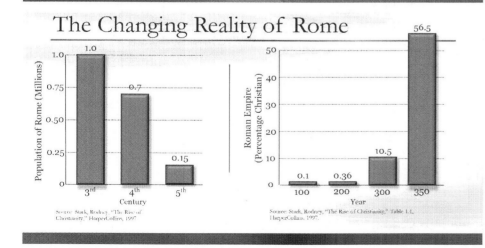

Source: Stark, Rodney, "The Rise of Christianity," HarperCollins, 1997.

Source: Stark, Rodney, "The Rise of Christianity," Table 1.1, HarperCollins, 1997.

A Sustainable Socioeconomic Model

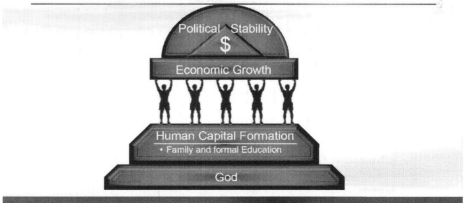

> The future of the world and of the Church passes through the family.
>
> Pope John Paul II
> *Familiaris Consortio, #75*

Small Group Discussion

Starter Questions

1. In what ways do you offer yourself in sacrifice for the purity of your spouse?
2. How do you manifest the Father who is rich in mercy to your children?

Next Week
The Death of the West

SESSION 11
The Death of the West

TMIY
THAT MAN IS YOU!
BECOMING A MAN AFTER GOD'S OWN HEART

Fulfilling Authentic Male Leadership

| Political Leadership | | Moral Leadership |
| Foundation for Future | | Personal Responsibility |

Sacrifice
The willingness to pay the price.

Economic Leadership		Military Leadership
Foundation for Future		Clarity of Thought
		Integrity of Action

A Sustainable Socioeconomic Model

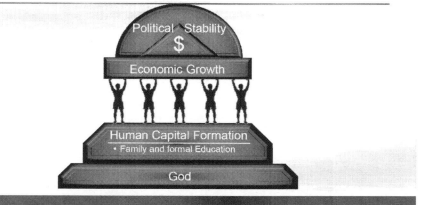

Political Stability
$
Economic Growth
Human Capital Formation
• Family and formal Education
God

The socioeconomic model that currently dominates Western culture attempts to remove God and the family from its foundation.

An Alternative Socioeconomic Model

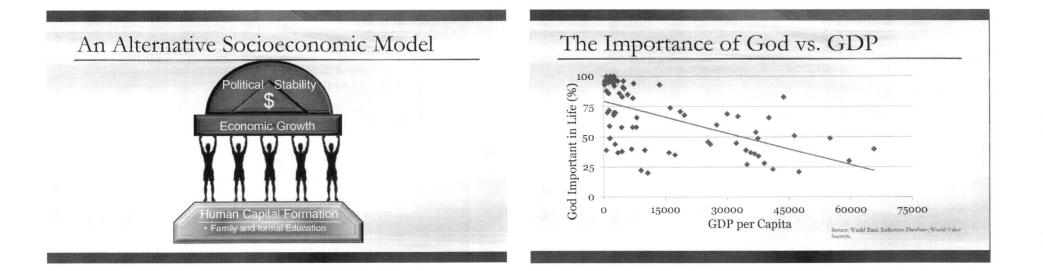

The Importance of God vs. GDP

Fertility vs. GDP

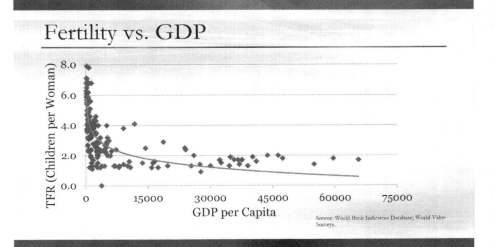

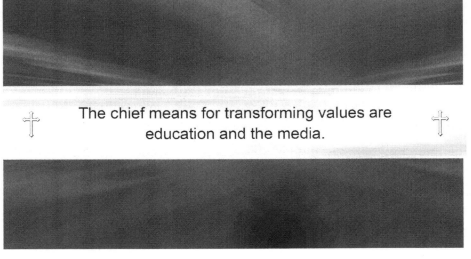

The chief means for transforming values are education and the media.

GDP per Capita vs. Education

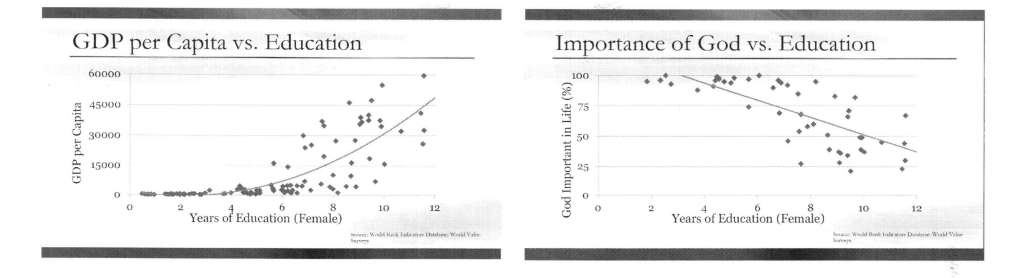

Fertility vs. Education

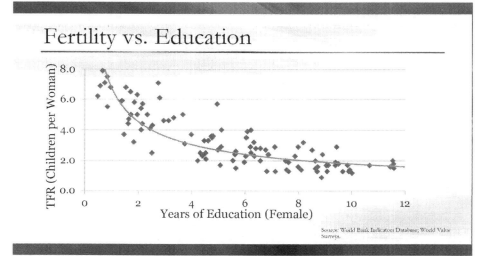

Importance of God vs. Education

First Marriage vs. Education

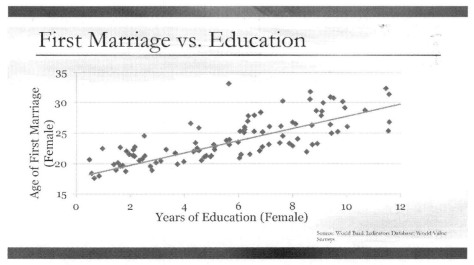

Source: World Bank Indicators Database; World Value Surveys

The Fertility Lifecycle of a Woman

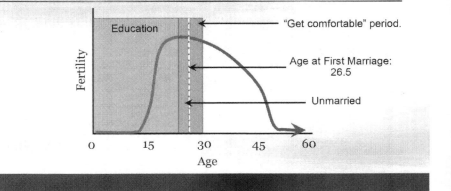

- "Get comfortable" period.
- Age at First Marriage: 26.5
- Unmarried

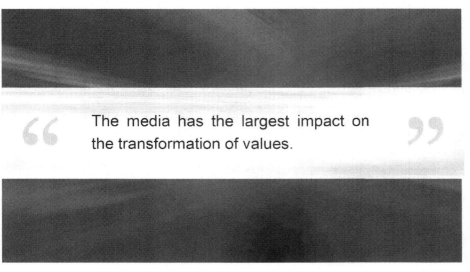

"The media has the largest impact on the transformation of values."

The Importance of God vs. Television

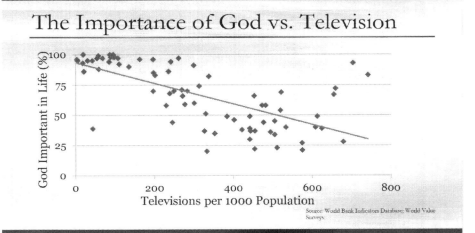

Source: World Bank Indicators Database; World Value Surveys.

Fertility vs. Television

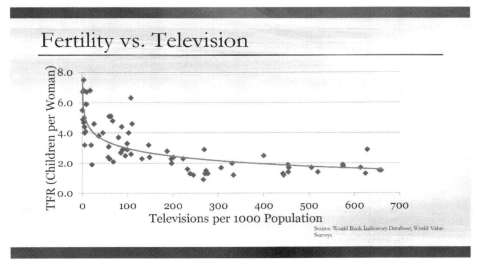

Source: World Bank Indicators Database; World Value Surveys.

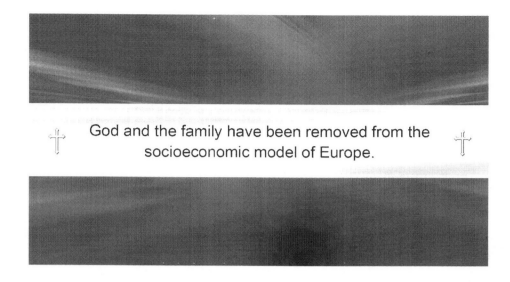

God and the family have been removed from the socioeconomic model of Europe.

The Secularization of Europe

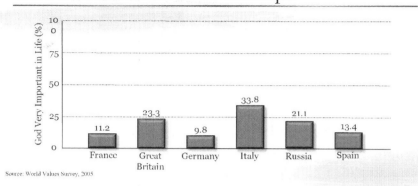

Source: World Values Survey, 2005

The Breakdown of the Family in Europe

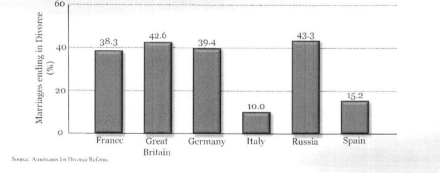

Source: Americans for Divorce Reform.

Total Fertility Rate in Europe

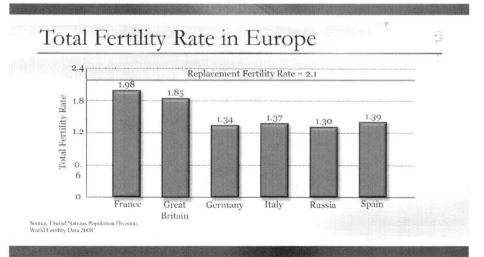

Source: United Nations Population Division, World Fertility Data 2008.

The Death of the European Culture

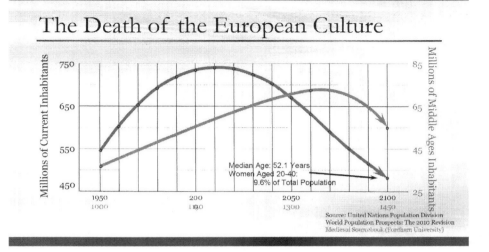

The Failed Leadership in Europe

- Personal Responsibility: < 10% go to Mass weekly.
- Clarity of Thought and Integrity of Action: Forty percent of marriages end in divorce.
- Foundation for the Future: Below replacement fertility rate.
- Pay the Price: The economic crises we see today are God's call to Europe.

One may legitimately ask whether [the socioeconomic system of the West] is not another form of totalitarianism, subtly concealed under the appearances of democracy ... communism fell in the end because of the system's socioeconomic weakness.

Pope John Paul II
Memory and Identity

Small Group Discussion

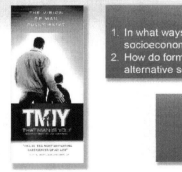

Starter Questions
1. In what ways have you accepted the alternative socioeconomic model?
2. How do form your children so that they don't accept the alternative socioeconomic model?

Next Week
The Cry of a Child

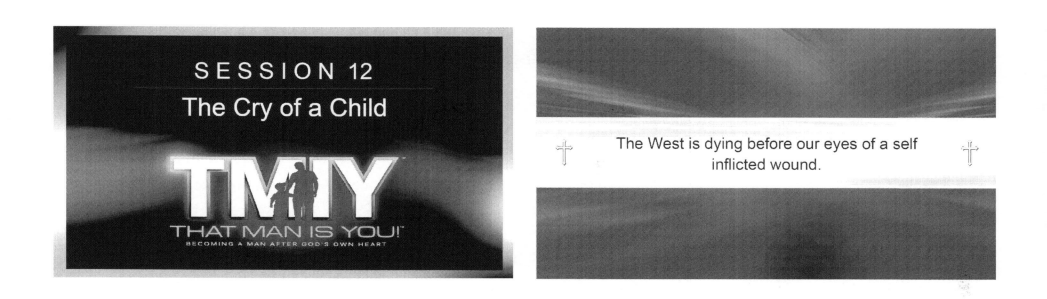

SESSION 12
The Cry of a Child

TMIY
THAT MAN IS YOU!
BECOMING A MAN AFTER GOD'S OWN HEART

The West is dying before our eyes of a self inflicted wound.

The Death of the European Culture

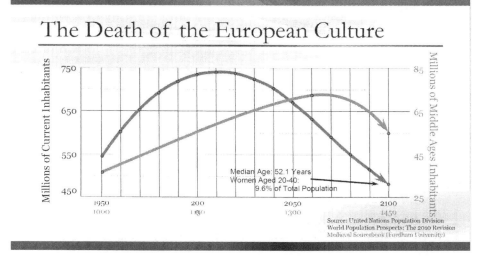

Median Age: 52.1 Years
Women Aged 20-40:
9.6% of Total Population

Source: United Nations Population Division
World Population Prospects: The 2010 Revision
Medieval Sourcebook (Fordham University)

The Failed Leadership in Europe

- Personal Responsibility: < 10% go to Mass weekly.
- Clarity of Thought and Integrity of Action: Forty percent of marriages end in divorce.
- Foundation for the Future: Below replacement fertility rate.
- Pay the Price: The economic crises we see today are God's call to Europe.

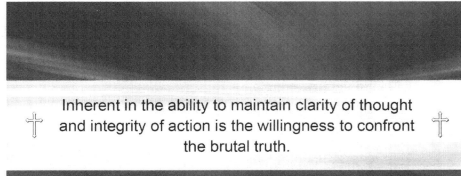

Inherent in the ability to maintain clarity of thought and integrity of action is the willingness to confront the brutal truth.

James Bond Stockdale

- 1923: Born on December 23rd.
- 1946: Graduates Naval Academy.
- 1962: Receives Master's Degree (Stanford)
- 1964: Leads first raid on Vietnam on August 6th.
- 1965: Shot down on September 9th.
- 1965-1973: Held as a POW in Vietnam.
- 1973ff: Receives Medal of Honor; 4 Silver Medals; 2 Purple Hearts; 2 Distinguished Flying Crosses; 3 Distinguished Service Medals.
- 2005: Dies on July 5th.

The Hanoi Hilton

- 1965-1973: POW in the "Hanoi Hilton."
- Highest ranking Naval officer to be captured.
- Solitary confinement for four years.
- Constrained in leg irons for two years.
- Tortured on 15 separate occasions.
- Broken back, dislocated shoulders, dislocated knee, hearing loss, malnourished.
- Disfigures face (cuts with razor and beats with stool leg) to avoid being a propaganda tool.
- Slits wrists to prove he will die rather than stop campaign to save fellow prisoners.
- Organizes POWs (rules of conduct during torture and communication code).

The Brutal Truth

"[Who didn't make it out?] The optimists. Oh, they were the ones who said, 'We're going to be out by Christmas.' And Christmas would come, and Christmas would go. Then they'd say, 'We're going to be out by Easter.' And Easter would come, and Easter would go. And then Thanksgiving, and then it would be Christmas again. And they died of a broken heart."

James Stockdale

The brutal truth is that modern men have succumbed to a temptation and our children are paying the price.

'You will not die. For God knows that when you eat of it your eyes will be opened, and you will be like God, knowing good and evil' ...When the woman saw that the tree was ... to be desired to make one wise, she took of its fruit and ate; and she also gave some to her husband, and he ate.

Genesis 3:1-5

And the eyes of them both were opened: and when they perceived themselves to be naked, they sewed together fig leaves, and made themselves clothes. And when they heard the voice of the Lord God walking in paradise at the afternoon air, Adam and his wife hid themselves from the face of the Lord God amidst the trees of paradise ... Cain rose up against his brother Abel, and killed him.

Genesis 3:7-4:8

The Enduring Temptation

A great portent appeared in heaven, a woman clothed with the sun, with the moon under her feet, and on her head a crown of twelve stars; she was with child and she cried out in her pangs of birth ... another portent appeared in heaven; behold, a great red dragon, with seven heads and ten horns ... And the dragon stood before the woman ... that he might devour her child when she brought it forth

Revelation 12:1-7

The Attack on Fatherhood

" … in human history the 'rays of fatherhood' meet a first resistance in the obscure but real fact of original sin. This is truly the key for interpreting reality … Original sin attempts, then, to abolish fatherhood. "

Pope John Paul II
Crossing the Threshold of Hope

The Faith of Fathers and Children

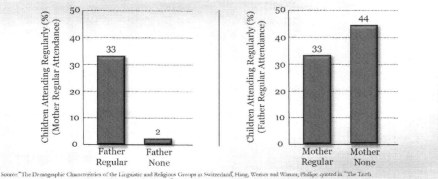

Source:"The Demographic Characteristics of the Linguistic and Religious Groups in Switzerland", Hang, Werner and Warner, Phillipe quoted in "The Truth about Men and Church: On the Importance of Fathers to Churchgoing," Low, Robbie, Touchstone Magazine, January/February, 2001.

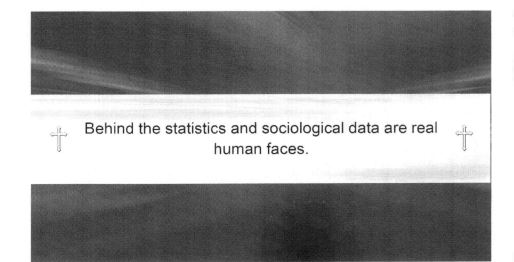

Behind the statistics and sociological data are real human faces.

Eminem

• Born Marshall Bruce Mathers III in 1972.

• Sold over 90 million albums – best selling artist of the 2000s.

• Won Academy Award for Best Song.

• Won 13 Grammy Awards including 3 consecutive Best Rap Album Grammys.

• Married/Divorce childhood sweetheart twice.

• Has one daughter – Halley Mathers.

• Took a several year hiatus associated with drug rehab in 2005.

• Resumed career with continued commercial success after 2009.

Eminem and his Father

- Abandoned by his father.
- Mother has a series of boyfriends.
- Lament over father: "My faggot father must had his panties up in a bunch. 'Cause he split. I wonder if he even kissed me good-bye.'"
- Troubled youth.
- Attempts suicide in 1999.
- Bond to his fans: "His f****** dad walkin' out."

Eminem: When I'm Gone

Eminem: When I'm Gone

What happens when you become the main source of her pain?
"Daddy look what I made", Dad's gotta go catch a plane.
"Daddy where's Mommy? I can't find Mommy where is she?"
I don't know go play Hailie, baby, your Daddy's busy.
Daddy's writing a song, this song ain't gonna write itself.
I'll give you one underdog then you gotta swing by yourself.
Baby, Daddy ain't leaving no more, "Daddy, you're lying
"You always say that, you always say this is the last time.
"But you ain't leaving no more, Daddy you're mine."
She's piling boxes in front of the door trying to block it.'
"Daddy please, Daddy don't leave, Daddy – no stop it!"

Eminem: When I'm Gone

I look up, it's just me standing in the mirror
These f—n' walls must be talking, cuz man I can hear 'em
They're say'n "You've got one more chance to do it right, and it's tonight."
Now go out there and show that you love 'em before it's too late
And just as I go to walk out of my bedroom door, it turns to a stage.
They're gone, and this spotlight is on and I'm singing ...
Sixty thousand people, all jumping out their seat.
The curtain closes, they're throwing roses at my feet.
I glance down, I don't believe what I'm seeing.

Eminem: When I'm Gone

"Daddy it's me, help Mommy, her wrists are bleeding."
But baby we're in Sweden, how did you get to Sweden?
"I followed you Daddy, you told me that you weren't leaven?
"You lied to me Dad, and now you make Mommy sad.
"And I brought you this coin, it says 'Number One Dad.'
"That's all I wanted, I just want to give you this coin.
"I get the point – fine. Me and Mommy are going."
But baby wait. "It's too late Dad, you made the choice.
"Now go out there and show 'em that you love 'em more than us.
I hear applause, all this time I couldn't see
How could it be, that the curtain is closing on me.
I turn around, find a gun on the ground, cock it
put it to my brain and scream "die Shaddy" and pop it.

Eminem: When I'm Gone

And when I'm gone, just carry on, don't mourn.
Rejoice every time you hear the sound of my voice.
Just know that I'm looking down on you smiling.
And I didn't feel a thing, so baby don't feel no pain.
Just smile back.
And when I'm gone, just carry on, don't mourn.
Rejoice every time you hear the sound of my voice.
Just know that I'm looking down on you smiling.
And I didn't feel a thing, so baby don't feel no pain.
Just smile back.

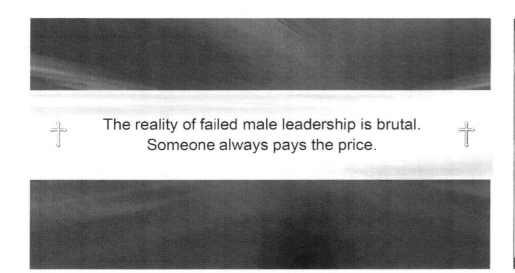

The reality of failed male leadership is brutal.
Someone always pays the price.

Small Group Discussion

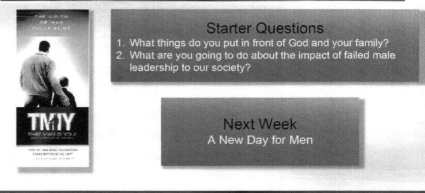

Starter Questions

1. What things do you put in front of God and your family?
2. What are you going to do about the impact of failed male leadership to our society?

Next Week
A New Day for Men

SESSION 13

A New Day for Men

TMIY

THAT MAN IS YOU!

BECOMING A MAN AFTER GOD'S OWN HEART

" The people who walked in darkness have seen a great light; upon those who dwelt in the land of gloom a light has shone. You have brought them abundant joy and great rejoicing ... for a child is born to us, a son is given us; upon his shoulder dominion rests. "

Isaiah 9:1-6
Midnight Mass, First Reading

" I see the dawning of a new missionary age, which will become a radiant day bearing an abundant harvest ... As the third millennium of the redemption draws near, God is preparing a great springtime for Christianity. "

Pope John Paul II
Redemptoris Missio, #92/#86

" The future of the world and of the Church passes through the family. "

Pope John Paul II
Familiaris Consortio, #75

The Population of Europe

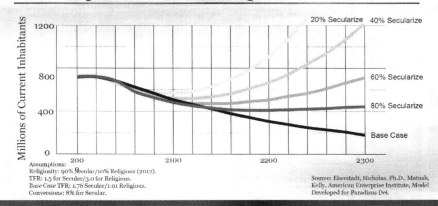

Millions of Current Inhabitants

20% Secularize   40% Secularize
60% Secularize
80% Secularize
Base Case

Assumptions:
Religiosity: 90% Secular/10% Religious (2012).
TFR: 1.5 for Secular/3.0 for Religious.
Base Case TFR: 1.76 Secular/1.91 Religious.
Conversions: 8% for Secular.

Source: Eberstadt, Nicholas, Ph.D., Matush, Kelly, American Enterprise Institute, Model Developed for Paradisus Dei.

The Religiosity of Europe

Percentage Religious

20% Secularize
40% Secularize
60% Secularize
80% Secularize
Base Case

Assumptions:
Religiosity: 90% Secular/10% Religious (2012).
TFR: 1.5 for Secular/3.0 for Religious.
Base Case TFR: 1.76 Secular/1.91 Religious.
Conversions: 8% for Secular.

Source: Eberstadt, Nicholas, Ph.D., Matush, Kelly, American Enterprise Institute, Model Developed for Paradisus Dei.

Fulfilling Authentic Male Leadership

Political Leadership
Foundation for Future

Moral Leadership
Personal Responsibility

Sacrifice
The willingness to pay the price.

Economic Leadership
Foundation for Future

Military Leadership
Clarity of Thought
Integrity of Action

Karol Jozef Wojtyla

- 1920: Born on May 18th.
- 1929: Mother dies.
- 1942: Enters underground seminary.
- 1944: Struck by German truck on February 29th.
- 1946: Ordained a priest on November 1st.
- 1958: Ordained a bishop on July 4th.
- 1967: Elevated to Cardinal on June 26th.
- 1978: Elected Pope on October 16th.
- 1981: Assassination attempt on May 13th.
- 2005: Dies on April 2nd (Vigil of Divine Mercy).

The Moral Leadership of John Paul II

- Pope John Paul I to Bishop John Magee: "He will come for I must go."
- Cardinal Stanislaw Dziwisz to Bishop John Magee: "Go and check the chapel again."
- Bishop John Magee: Pope John Paul II is a man of profound prayer.
- Pope John Paul II went to confession every Friday that he was in Rome.

The Military Leadership of John Paul II

- "The family is placed at the heart of the great struggle between good and evil, between life and death, between love and all that is opposed to love" (*Letter to Families*, #23).
- Began Pontificate with catechesis on the meaning of marriage (Theology of the Body).
- Established the Pontifical Council of the Family, the Pope John Paul II Institute on Marriage and Family, and the World Meetings of Family.

The Economic Leadership of John Paul II

- "Communism fell in the end because of the system's socioeconomic weakness" (*Memory and Identity*, p. 48).
- "The primary basis of the value of work is man himself ... in the final analysis it is always man who is the purpose of the work, whatever work it is that is done by man – even if the common scale of values rates it as the merest 'service'" (Laborem Exercens, #6).

The Political Leadership of John Paul II

- "The pope started this chain of events that led to the end of communism" (Lech Walesa).
- "At the dawn of the new millennium, we wish to propose once more the message of hope which comes from the stable of Bethlehem: God loves all men and women on earth and gives them the hope of a new era, an era of peace. His love, fully revealed in the Incarnate Son, is the foundation of universal peace" (World Day of Peace, January 1, 2000).

As an authentic leader, Pope John Paul II was willing to pay the price until the very end.

A Sacrifice for the Family

"I understood that I must lead Christ's Church into this third millennium through suffering … Precisely because the family is threatened, the family is under attack. The Pope has to be attacked, the Pope has to suffer, so that every family and the world may see that there is … a higher Gospel … by which the future is prepared, the third millennium of families" (May 29, 1994).

John Paul II and the First Word

- "Father forgive them, for they know not what they do" (Luke 23:34).
- "Grant that our forebears, our brothers and sisters, and we, your servants, who by the grace of the Holy Spirit turn back to you in whole-hearted repentance, may experience your mercy and receive the forgiveness of our sins" (March 12, 2000).
- Pope John Paul II took personal responsibilities for his actions and those of the whole Church.

John Paul II and the Second Word

- "Today you will be with me in Paradise" (Luke 23:43).
- "God, clearly represented by the father in the parable [of the prodigal son], welcomes every prodigal child that returns to him" (March 12, 2000).
- Pope John Paul II maintained clarity of thought about humanity's eternal destiny.

John Paul II and the Third Word

- "Woman, behold your son. [Disciple], behold your mother" (John 19:26).
- "Therefore, O Mother, like the Apostle John, we wish to take you into our home, that we may learn from you to become like your Son. 'Woman, behold your Son.' Here we stand before you to entrust to your maternal care ourselves, the Church, the entire world ... grant that ... the darkness will not prevail over the light. To you, Dawn of Salvation, we commit our journey through the new Millennium" (October 8, 2000).
- Pope John Paul II laid a foundation for the future.

John Paul II and the Fourth Word

- "My God, my God, why have you forsaken me?" (Matthew 27:46).
- "Now, however, [God] seems absent, as though asleep or indifferent. He feeds the flock he must lead and nourish only with the bread of tears. Enemies scoff at this humiliated, despised people; yet God does not seem to be moved nor 'to be stirred up' ... (T)his is the Psalmist's conviction that finds an echo in our hearts and opens them to hope" (April 10, 2002).
- Pope John Paul II felt the apparent abandonment of God. He was willing to pay the price.

John Paul II and the Fifth Word

- "I thirst" (John 19:28).
- "I find great peace in thinking of the time when the Lord will call me: from life to life! And so I often find myself saying, with no trace of melancholy, a prayer recited by priests after the celebration of the Eucharist ... at the hour of my death, call me and bid me come to you" (Letter to the Elderly, October 1, 1999).
- Pope John Paul II maintained clarity of thought about his own destiny.

John Paul II and the Sixth Word

- "Father, into your hands I commend my spirit" (Luke 23:46).
- "He has surrender himself to God" (Spokesman for Pope John Paul II, April 1, 2005).
- Pope John Paul II lived integrity of action, surrendering himself fully to God.

John Paul II and the Seventh Word

- "It is consummated" (John 19:30).
- "Amen." (The last word spoken by Pope John Paul II on April 2, 2005).
- Pope John Paul II lived integrity of action until the end.

Remaining steadfastly united to God, authentic leaders receive the blessings of God and experience an incredible fruitfulness.

The Focus upon the Great Jubilee

"This time, in which God in His hidden design has entrusted to me … the universal service connected with the Chair of St. Peter in Rome, is already very close to the year 2000 … We also are in a certain way in a season of new Advent, a season of new expectation.

Redemptoris Hominis #1

Crossing the Threshold of Hope

"But certainly 'a river of living water' … has been poured out on the Church. This is the water of the Spirit which quenches thirst and brings new life … Christ whom we have contemplated and loved bids us to set out once more on our journey … we can count on the power of the same Holy Spirit who was poured out at Pentecost and who impels us still today to start out anew."

Novo Millennio Ineunte #1 and #57

The Triumph of Mercy

"To humanity, which at times seems to be lost and dominated by the power of evil, egotism and fear, the risen Lord offers as a gift his love that forgives, reconciles and reopens the spirit to hope. It is love that converts hearts and gives peace. How much need the world has to understand and accept Divine Mercy. Lord, who with [your] Death and Resurrection reveal the love of the Father, we believe in you and with confidence repeat to you today: Jesus, I trust in You, have mercy on us and on the whole world."

April 3, 2005.

Small Group Discussion

Starter Questions
1. How can you become an apostle of the new springtime of the Church?
2. Who are you going to bring with you to the program in January?

See you in January

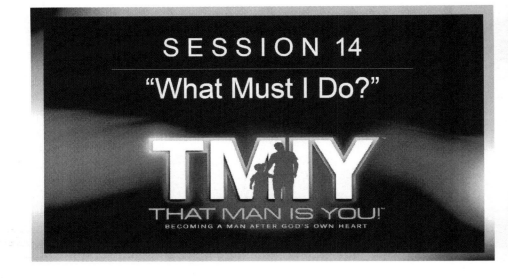

SESSION 14

"What Must I Do?"

TMIY

THAT MAN IS YOU!

BECOMING A MAN AFTER GOD'S OWN HEART

✝ That Man is You! is about authentic male leadership. We began our journey considering the current state of male leadership. ✝

Trading Energy Derivatives

- Very high risk.
- Market dominated by factors beyond control.
- Difficult financial instrument to trade.
- Attractive to intelligent men who love challenge.
- Traders conversant on current affairs.
- Opportunity for large financial rewards.
- Incredibly pagan environment.

To be "A Good Guy"

- Trader claims to be "a good guy."
- No one agrees.
- Selection of Ten Commandments as an objective standard.
- No one can name Ten Commandments.
- Public examination of conscience.
- Claimed 3½ out of ten. Actually 2 for 10.
- Average of traders was 2½ out of 10.

The "Knock of God"

- The trader was visibly shaken by the results.
- God knocked on the trader's heart that day.
- The prophet was a declared atheist.
- "I wished I could be like you, but we can't all live our lives like you."
- He never changed his life.
- Many of the trader's said the same thing. They didn't change their life.
- "What would Steve do?"

The Saddest Story in the Gospel (Mark 10:17-22)

- "Good Teacher: what must I do to inherit everlasting life?"
- "You know the commandments."
- "All these I have observed from my youth."
- "Jesus looking upon him loved him, 'You lack one thing: go, sell what you have, and give to the poor, and you will have treasure in heaven; and come, follow me.'"
- "At this saying his countenance fell, and he went away sorrowful."

 Jesus Christ personally invited you to be here today. You said, 'Yes.' And I thank you.

 Wherever you are in your spiritual life, Jesus Christ wants to encounter you right there … and take you further.

> *That Man is You! is about a personal encounter with Jesus Christ so that Jesus Christ can transform your life.*

The Path of Transformation

> *Turn away from sin and be faithful to the Gospel (Ash Wednesday Liturgy).*

That Man is You!

Fall Semester

- Identified the four leadership roles of men.
- Identified the five personal characteristics of authentic leaders.
- Made an honest assessment of the current state of male leadership.
- Considered the consequences of failed male leadership.
- Was more theological.

Becoming a Man after God's own Heart

Spring Semester

- Considers where and how we can be transformed in to authentic leaders.
- Considers the primary temptations of Satan and the means for conquering them.
- Considers the means for living in union with God – from whom all authentic leadership flows.

Becoming a Man after God's own Heart

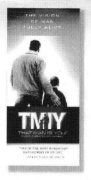

Spring Semester

- We'll understand the three primary sacraments that will aid in this union.
- We'll learn to live by the "three covenants" of the Church.
- We'll put a plan of action in place to help us develop the personal characteristics necessary to embrace our leadership roles.
- It will be more action oriented.

The Tools at our Disposal

The Three Wisdoms

- The best research from secular science (especially medical and social science).
- The teachings of our faith (based upon Scripture, Tradition and the teachings of the Magisterium).
- The wisdom of the saints handed down through the centuries.

> The Spirit of the Lord shall rest upon him: the spirit of wisdom and understanding, the spirit of counsel and fortitude, the spirit of knowledge and piety. And his delight shall be in the fear of the Lord.
>
> Isaiah 11:2-3

> There were no dry eyes this morning. That alone should tell you the effect this program has had on our men ... So many lives have been changed for the better. So many marriages have been turned around. So many addictions have been set aside ... I could go on and on ... It was evident they didn't want this moment to end.
>
> Core Team Leader ⊠ Florida

Small Group Discussion

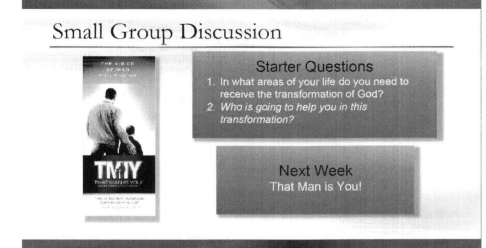

Starter Questions

1. In what areas of your life do you need to receive the transformation of God?
2. *Who is going to help you in this transformation?*

Next Week
That Man is You!

SESSION 15

That Man is You!

TMIY

THAT MAN IS YOU!
BECOMING A MAN AFTER GOD'S OWN HEART

✝ The consequences to failed male leadership are dramatic not only to ourselves, but also to greater society. ✝

The Story of King David

- Chosen by God and consecrated as King of Israel by the Prophet Samuel.
- Commits adultery with Bathsheba, who becomes pregnant with his child.
- Arranges for the death of Bathsheba's husband, Uriah.
- Takes Bathsheba for his wife.
- Confronted by the Prophet Nathan who tells David the parable of the two men.

The Consequences for King David

1. Disharmony in the Family
"I will take your wives while you live to see it" (2 Samuel 12:11).

2. Children will Suffer
"The child that is born to you shall die" (2 Samuel 12:14).

3. Conflict in Society
"The sword shall not depart from your house" (2 Samuel 12:10).

4. Worship of God will Suffer
"David may not build a house for my name for he is a man of war and has shed blood" (1 Chronicles 22:8).

Male Sexual Infidelity

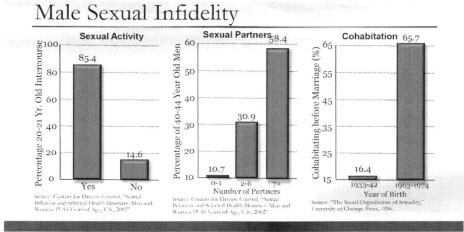

Sexual Activity

Percentage 20-21 Yr. Old Intercourse

- 85.4 — Yes
- 14.6 — No

Source: Centers for Disease Control, "Sexual Behavior and Selected Health Measures: Men and Women 15-44 Years of Age, U.S., 2002"

Sexual Partners

Percentage of 40-44 Year Old Men

- 0-1: 10.7
- 2-6: 30.9
- 7+: 58.4

Number of Partners

Source: Centers for Disease Control, "Sexual Behavior and Selected Health Measures: Men and Women 15-44 Years of Age, U.S., 2002"

Cohabitation

Cohabitating before Marriage (%)

- 1933-42: 16.4
- 1963-1974: 65.7

Year of Birth

Source: "The Social Organization of Sexuality," University of Chicago Press, 1994.

Disharmony in the Family

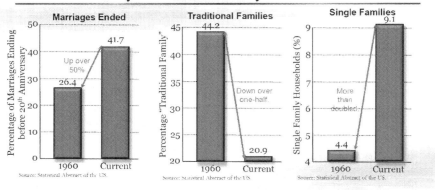

Marriages Ended

Percentage of Marriages Ending before 20th Anniversary

- 1960: 26.4
- Current: 41.7

Up over 50%

Source: Statistical Abstract of the US.

Traditional Families

Percentage "Traditional Family"

- 1960: 44.2
- Current: 20.9

Down over one-half.

Source: Statistical Abstract of the US

Single Families

Single Family Households (%)

- 1960: 4.4
- Current: 9.1

More than doubled.

Source: Statistical Abstract of the US.

The Children will Suffer

Abortions

Percentage of Conceptions Aborted

- 1960: <1
- Current: ~22

Exploded.

Source: Statistical Abstract of the US

Illegitimate Births

Percentage Illegitimate Births

- 1960: 5.3
- Current: 40.7

Up 7.5 TIMES.

Source: Statistical Abstract of the US, Vital Statistics of the US.

Divorce

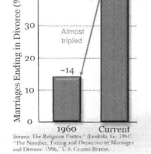

Marriages Ending in Divorce (%)

- 1960: ~14
- Current: ~40

Almost tripled.

Source: "The Religious Factor," (Lenksi, G. 1961), "The Number, Timing and Duration of Marriages and Divorce, 1996," U.S. Census Bureau.

Conflict in Society

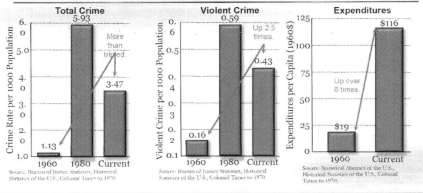

Total Crime

Crime Rate per 1000 Population

- 1960: 1.13
- 1980: 5.93
- Current: 3.47

More than tripled.

Source: Bureau of Justice Statistics, Historical Statistics of the U.S., Colonial Times to 1970

Violent Crime

Violent Crime per 1000 Population

- 1960: 0.16
- 1980: 0.59
- Current: 0.43

Up 2.5 times.

Source: Bureau of Justice Statistics, Historical Statistics of the U.S., Colonial Times to 1970

Expenditures

Expenditures per Capita (1960$)

- 1960: $19
- Current: $116

Up over 6 times.

Source: Statistical Abstract of the U.S., Historical Statistics of the U.S., Colonial Times to 1970.

The Worship of God will Suffer

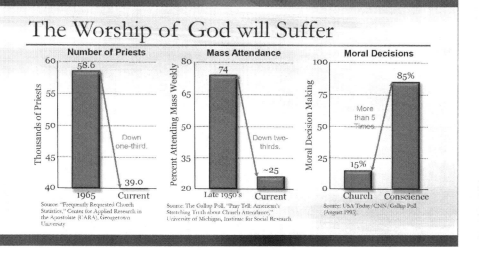

Number of Priests

Thousands of Priests

58.6 (1965)
Down one-third.
39.0 (Current)

Source: "Frequently Requested Church Statistics," Center for Applied Research in the Apostolate (CARA), Georgetown University

Mass Attendance

Percent Attending Mass Weekly

74 (Late 1950's)
Down two-thirds.
~25 (Current)

Source: The Gallup Poll, "Pray Tell: American's Stretching Truth about Church Attendance," University of Michigan, Institute for Social Research.

Moral Decisions

Moral Decision Making

15% (Church)
More than 5 Times
85% (Conscience)

Source: USA Today/CNN/Gallup Poll (August 1993).

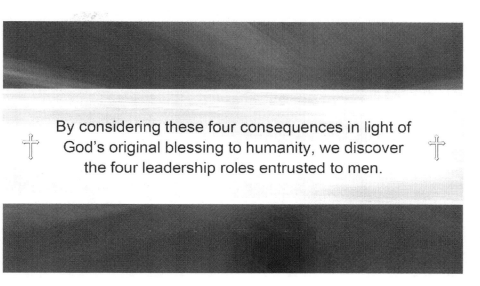

By considering these four consequences in light of God's original blessing to humanity, we discover the four leadership roles entrusted to men.

And God blessed them saying, 'Increase and multiply and fill the earth and subdue it. And have dominion over the fishes of the sea and the fowls of the air and all the creatures that move upon the earth.

Genesis 1:28

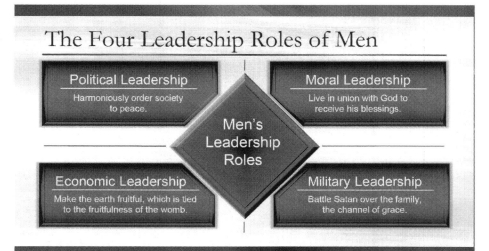

The Four Leadership Roles of Men

Political Leadership
Harmoniously order society to peace.

Moral Leadership
Live in union with God to receive his blessings.

Men's Leadership Roles

Economic Leadership
Make the earth fruitful, which is tied to the fruitfulness of the womb.

Military Leadership
Battle Satan over the family, the channel of grace.

The Relationship between God and Marriage

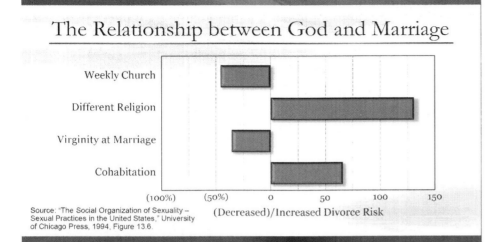

Weekly Church
Different Religion
Virginity at Marriage
Cohabitation

(100%) (50%) 0 50 100 150

(Decreased)/Increased Divorce Risk

Source: "The Social Organization of Sexuality –
Sexual Practices in the United States," University
of Chicago Press, 1994, Figure 13.6.

Marriage and Physical Fruitfulness

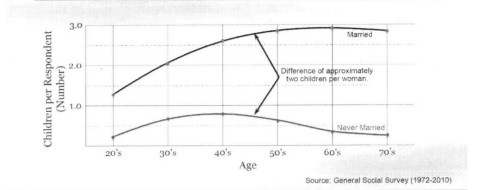

Children per Respondent (Number)

3.0
2.0
1.0

20's 30's 40's 50's 60's 70's

Age

Married

Difference of approximately
two children per woman.

Never Married

Source: General Social Survey (1972-2010)

Marriage and Economic Fruitfulness

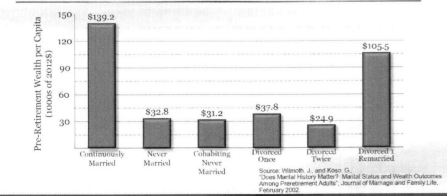

Pre-Retirement Wealth per Capita (1000s of 2012$)

150
120
90
60
30

$139.2

$32.8 $31.2 $37.8 $24.9

$105.5

Continuously
Married
Never
Married
Cohabiting
Never
Married
Divorced
Once
Divorced
Twice
Divorced /
Remarried

Source: Wilmoth, J., and Koso, G.,
"Does Marital History Matter? Marital Status and Wealth Outcomes
Among Preretirement Adults", Journal of Marriage and Family Life,
February 2002.

Marriage and Peace and Happiness

- Married couples are 60% more likely to be happy with their lives.
- Married couples have more frequent sex.
- Church going spouses are 22% more likely to be sexually satisfied than non-church going spouses.
- Divorce significantly increases depression and triples the likelihood a person will commit suicide.
- Divorced people are 2.5X more likely than married persons to be unhappy with their lives.

Source: Waite, Linda J. and Gallagher, Maggie, "The Case for Marriage – Why Married
People are Happier, Healthier and Better Off Financially," Doubleday, 2000.

A Sustainable Socioeconomic Model

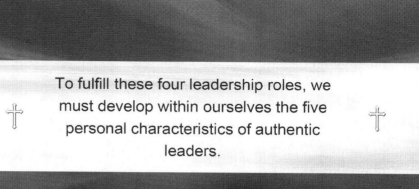

To fulfill these four leadership roles, we must develop within ourselves the five personal characteristics of authentic leaders.

Fulfilling Authentic Male Leadership

Clarity of Thought for Men

- God is found in communion.
- "Where two or three are gathered in my name, there am I in the midst of them" (Matthew 18:20).
- "Whoever receives one such child in my name receives me" (Matthew 18:5).

Integrity of Action

- We must unite ourselves to Christ so that we may gain possession of ourselves.
- We must unite our marriages to Christ so that they can withstand the storms of time.
- We must unite our children to Christ so that they may attain to the full stature of Christ.

To Pay the Price

- Sacrifice lays at the foundation of each of the other four authentic leadership traits.
- Fully embraced, sacrifice transforms leadership into authentic Christian leadership.
- "Husbands, love your wives, as Christ loved the church and gave himself up for her … that he might present the church to himself in splendor, without spot or wrinkle or any such thing" (Ephesians 5:25-27).

Well lived, these five traits transform us into authentic leaders and they transform our homes into the foundation for an authentically Christian culture.

Small Group Discussion

Starter Questions

1. Which of the four leadership roles is most difficult for you to embrace?
2. Which of the five personal traits of leaders do you most need to develop in your life?

Next Week
The Battle over Fatherhood

SESSION 16

The Heart of Man

TMIY

THAT MAN IS YOU!

BECOMING A MAN AFTER GOD'S OWN HEART

We have painted a pretty dim picture of the current state of men in our society. Does this picture reflect the reality of a man's heart?

A Divine Lesson for the Heart of Man

"The first meaning of man's original solitude is defined on the basis of a specific test, or examination, which man undergoes before God (and in a certain way also before himself) ... Man is not only essentially and subjectively alone. Solitude, in fact, also signifies man's subjectivity, which is constituted through self-knowledge. Man is alone because he is 'different' from the visible world."

Pope John Paul II
October 10, 1979

The Heart is Larger than Sensual Pleasure

"The Lord God formed man of dust from the ground, and breathed into his nostrils the breath of life: and man became a living being. And the Lord God planted a garden in Eden, in the east; and there he put the man whom he had formed. And out of the ground the Lord God made to grow every tree that is pleasant to the sight and good for food.

Genesis 2:7-9

The Heart is Larger than Work

> The Lord God took the man and put him in the garden of Eden to till it and keep it ... Then the Lord God said, 'It is not good that the man should be alone; I will make a helper fit for him.'
>
> Genesis 2:15-18

The Heart is Larger than Domination

> So out of the ground the Lord God formed every beast of the field and every bird of the air, and brought them to the man to see what he would call them; and whatever the man called every living creature, that was its name ... but for the man there was not found a helper fit for him.
>
> Genesis 2:19-20

The Moment of Self-Consciousness

"Through this 'test,' man gains the consciousness of his own superiority, that is, that he cannot be put on a par with any other species of living beings on the earth ... With this knowledge, which makes him go in some way outside of his own being, man at the same time reveals himself to himself in all the distinctiveness of his being ... Man is alone because he is 'different' from the visible world, from the world of living beings."

Pope John Paul II
October 10, 1979

The Thirst of the Human Heart

- "God created man in his own image, in the image of God he created him; male and female he created them" (Genesis 1:27).
- "I thirst" (John 19:28).
- "He who has seen me has seen the Father" (John 14:9).
- "Men relive and reveal on earth the very fatherhood of God" (Pope John Paul II, Familiaris Consortio, #25).

The Fulfillment of the Heart's Desires

"So the Lord God caused a deep sleep to fall upon the man, and while he slept took one of his ribs and closed up its place with flesh; and the rib with the Lord God had taken from the man he made into a woman and brought her to the man. Then the man said, 'This at last is bone of my bones and flesh of my flesh; she shall be called Woman, because she was taken out of Man.' Therefore a man leaves his father and his mother and cleaves to his wife, and they become one flesh" (Genesis 2:21-24).

The Renewal of Creation

- "When they unite with each other (in the conjugal act) so closely as to become 'one flesh,' man and woman rediscover every time, and in a special way, the mystery of creation" (Pope John Paul II, November 21, 1979).
- "I have gotten a man with the help of the Lord" (Genesis 4:1).
- "Some propagate and conserve the spiritual life in a spiritual ministry only … some belong to the bodily and spiritual life simultaneously" (St. Thomas Aquinas).

There is someone who does not rejoice in the revelation of a creature created to "the image and likeness of God" – Satan.

The "Heart" of the Devil

- Satan is created as a "good angel".
- Satan is called to serve humanity: "Are angels not all ministering spirits sent forth to serve, for the sake of those who are to obtain salvation" (Hebrews 1:14)?
- Satan is envious of man: "[Satan] because of the many gifts of God, which He gave to the man, became jealous and looked on him with envy" (St. Irenaeus, *On Apostolic Teaching*, #16).
- Satan rejects mission: "I will not serve" (Jeremiah 2:20).

The Fall of Satan

- "You were blameless in your way till iniquity was found in you ... Your heart was proud because of your beauty; you corrupted your wisdom for the sake of your splendor" (Ezekiel 28:15-17).
- "How are you fallen from heaven ... you said 'I will ascend above the heights of the clouds; I will make myself like the Most High.' But you are brought down to Sheol, to the depths of the Pit" (Isaiah 14:12-15).
- Satan sets himself in opposition to God.

The Temptation and Fall of Humanity

"The serpent was more subtle than any other wild creature that the Lord God had made. He said to the woman, 'Did God say, 'You shall not eat of any tree of the garden?' ... You will not die. For God knows that when you eat of it your eyes will be opened, and you will be like God, knowing good and evil.' When the woman saw that the tree was ... to be desired to make one wise, she took of its fruit and ate; and she also gave some to her husband, and he ate."

Genesis 3:1-6

The Shrinking of the Human Heart

"And the eyes of them both were opened: and when they perceived themselves to be naked, they sewed together fig leaves, and made themselves clothes. And when they heard the voice of the Lord God walking in paradise at the afternoon air, Adam and his wife hid themselves from the face of the Lord God amidst the trees of paradise."

Genesis 3:7-8

The Attack on Fatherhood

"... in human history the 'rays of fatherhood' meet a first resistance in the obscure but real fact of original sin. This is truly the key for interpreting reality ... Original sin attempts, then, to abolish fatherhood."

Pope John Paul II
Crossing the Threshold of Hope

The Darkness of the World

- "God drove out the man; and at the east of the garden of Eden he placed the cherubim, and a flaming sword which turned every way, to guard the way to the tree of life" (Genesis 3:24).
- "All that is in the world, the concupiscence of the flesh, the concupiscence of the eyes and the pride of life, is not of the Father but is of the world" (1 John 2:16).

God turns Satan's apparent victory upon itself. It becomes the means by which God gives humanity another divine lesson. We learn that the "Father is rich in mercy" (Ephesians 2:4).

A "New Encounter" with the Father

- "Have I any pleasure in the death of the wicked, says the Lord God, and not rather that he should turn from his way and live" (Ezekiel 18:23).
- "For God so loved the world that he gave his only Son, that whoever believes in him should not perish but have eternal life. For God sent the Son into the world, not to condemn the world, but that he world might be saved through him" (John 3:16-17).
- The Father "is rich in mercy" (Ephesians 2:4).

The Repentance of King David

" Have mercy on me, O God according to thy steadfast love; according to thy abundant mercy blot out my transgressions … Against thee, thee only, have I sinned, and done that which is evil in thy sight, so that thou art justified in thy sentence and blameless in thy judgment … Create in me a clean heart, O God, and put a new and right spirit within me. Cast me not away from thy presence … O Lord, open thou my lips, and my mouth shall show forth thy praise. For thou hast no delight in sacrifice … The sacrifice acceptable to God is a broken spirit; a broken and contrite heart, O God, thou wilt not despise. "

Psalm 51:1-17

A Man after God's own Heart

"[God] raised up David to be their king; of whom he testified and said, 'I have found in David the son of Jesse, a man after my heart, who will do all my will.' Of this man's posterity God has brought to Israel a Savior, Jesus, as he promised."

Acts 13:22-23

King David became a "man after God's own heart" not because he was innocent of sin, but because having sinned, he encountered the Father, rich in mercy, and allowed him to expand his heart to all that it was created to be.

Small Group Discussion

Starter Questions
1. In what ways does Satan try to shrink your heart to make it less than it was created to be?
2. In what ways can you allow the Father to expand your heart to be everything that it was created to be?

Next Week
Becoming a Man after God's own Heart

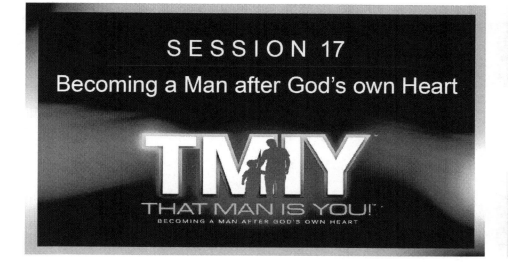

SESSION 17

Becoming a Man after God's own Heart

TMIY

THAT MAN IS YOU!

BECOMING A MAN AFTER GOD'S OWN HEART

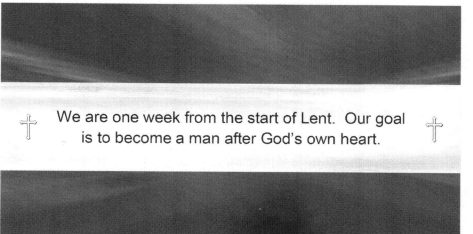

✝ We are one week from the start of Lent. Our goal is to become a man after God's own heart. ✝

The Parable of the Sower and the Seed

" A sower went out to sow … the seed is the Word of God.

Matthew 13:3 and Luke 8:11 "

The First Seed: The Devil Steals

- **The Parable:**
"Some seeds fell along the path, and the birds came and devoured them" (Matthew 13:4).
- **Christ's Explanation:**
"When one hears the word of the kingdom and does not understand it, the evil one comes and snatches away what was sown in his heart" (Matthew 13:19).
- **The Reality:**
A heart that is not united to God.

The Second Seed: Lack of Depth in Self

- **The Parable:**
  "Other seeds fell on rocky ground, where they had not much soil, and immediately they sprang up, since they had no depth of soil, but when the sun rose they were scorched; and since they had no root they withered away" (Matthew 13:5-6).
- **Christ's Explanation:**
  "He who hears word and immediately receives it with joy; yet he has no root in himself, but endures for awhile and when tribulation or persecution arises on account of the word, immediately he falls away" (Matthew 13:20-21).
- **The Reality:**
  A heart that is a slave to the comforts of this world.

The Third Seed: Deceived by Riches

- **The Parable:**
  "Other seeds fell upon thorns, and the thorns grew up and chocked them" (Matthew 13:7).
- **Christ's Explanation:**
  "This is he who hears the word, but the cares of the world and the delight in riches choke the word, and it proves unfruitful" (Matthew 13:22).
- **The Reality:**
  A heart that is bound by this world.

The Fourth Seed: The Good Soil

- **The Parable:**
  "Other seeds fell on good soil and brought forth grain, some a hundredfold, some sixty, some thirty." (Matthew 13:8).
- **Christ's Explanation:**
  "This is he who hears the word and understands it; he indeed bears fruit, and yields, in one case a hundredfold, in another sixty, and in another thirty" (Matthew 13:23).
- **The Reality:**
  A heart that experiences superabundance in God.

The first three types of soil help us to understand the three basic orientations in the spiritual life and Satan's three fundamental temptations of the soul.

The Three Fundamental Orientations

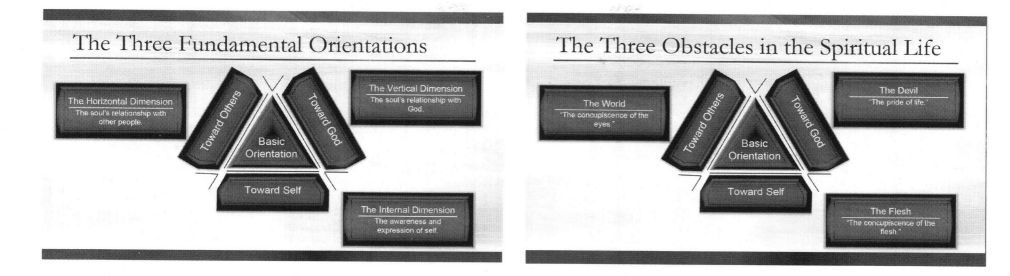

The Three Obstacles in the Spiritual Life

Our goal is to unite ourselves securely to Christ so that he can expand our heart to be all that it was created to be.

The That Man is You! Lenten Journey

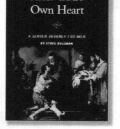

- Helps each man evaluate his spiritual life through the aid of three exercises.
- Helps each man understand the steps he can take to avoid the temptations of Satan.
- Helps each man understand the pathway to union with God according to three practices.
- Helps each man put a plan of life in place to "become a man after God's own heart."

Lenten Dates

Ash Wednesday to Holy Saturday

2017: March 1 - April 15

2018: February 14 - March 30

2019: March 6 - April 20

2020: February 26 - April 11

2021: February 17 - April 13

The Forty Days of Lent

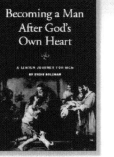

- Days from Ash Wednesday to Holy Saturday.
- Does NOT include Sundays – the day of the Lord's Resurrection.
- Ash Wednesday and Good Friday are days of fast (1 meal plus two snacks) and abstinence (no meat).
- Fridays are days of abstinence (no meat).
- All days (except Sunday) are days of penance.

The Daily Lenten Program

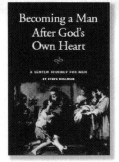

1. Begin the day with a consecration of the day and ourselves to God.
2. Daily exercise to help us overcome the obstacles in the spiritual life and encounter God.
3. Daily sacrifice designed to coordinate with the daily exercise.
4. Brief examination of conscience at the end of the day.

The Weeks of Lent

- Forty days of Lent are spread across 6 ½ weeks.
- Week of Ash Wednesday (½ week).
- First week of Lent; Second week of Lent; Third week of Lent; Fourth week of Lent; Fifth week of Lent.
- Holy Week

The Weekly Lenten Program

1. Orientation: We will consider each of the three fundamental orientations twice.
2. Exercise (performed daily): designed to help the soul "turn away from sin and be faithful to the Gospel."
3. Sacrifice: We will make a sacrifice each week that reinforces the exercise.
4. Covenant: We will put in place a covenant that helps us live our spiritual exercise.

The That Man is You! Lenten Journey has three exercises designed to help you personally evaluate how Satan attempts to disrupt your spiritual life.

The Three Exercises of That Man is You!

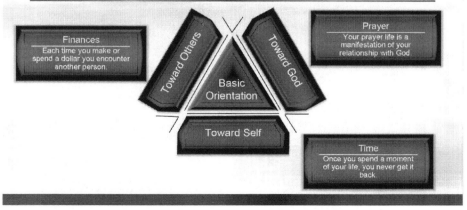

The That Man is You! Lenten Journey will also help you put into place practices that will allow you to encounter God according to each of your three fundamental orientations.

Encountering God

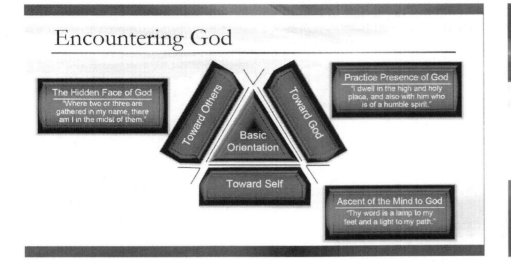

The Hidden Face of God
"Where two or three are gathered in my name, there am I in the midst of them."

Toward Others

Toward God

Basic Orientation

Toward Self

Practice Presence of God
"I dwell in the high and holy place, and also with him who is of a humble spirit."

Ascent of the Mind to God
"Thy word is a lamp to my feet and a light to my path."

✝ Over all these we will put on mercy so that we may truly become a manifestation of the Father "who is rich in mercy" (Ephesians 2:4). ✝

Small Group Discussion

Starter Questions
1. Which of the three fundamental temptations of Satan is most difficult for you and why?
2. When are you going to set aside time in your schedule for your Lenten exercises?

Next Week
A Heart Enslaved by the Flesh

SESSION 18

A Heart Enslaved by the Flesh

TMIY

THAT MAN IS YOU!

BECOMING A MAN AFTER GOD'S OWN HEART

To "become a man after God's own heart" we must not allow our hearts to be shrunk by "the concupiscence of the flesh, the concupiscence of the eyes or the pride of life.

The Daily Lenten Program

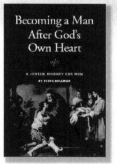

Becoming a Man After God's Own Heart

A LENTEN JOURNEY FOR MEN

BY STEVE BOLLMAN

1. Begin the day with a consecration of the day and ourselves to God.
2. Daily exercise to help us overcome the obstacles in the spiritual life and encounter God.
3. Daily sacrifice designed to coordinate with the daily exercise.
4. Brief examination of conscience at the end of the day.

The Weekly Lenten Program

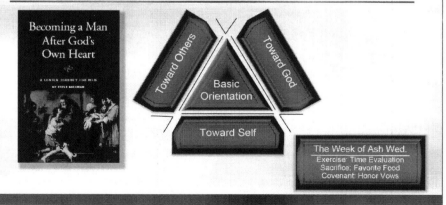

Becoming a Man After God's Own Heart

A LENTEN JOURNEY FOR MEN

BY STEVE BOLLMAN

Toward Others

Toward God

Basic Orientation

Toward Self

The Week of Ash Wed.
Exercise: Time Evaluation
Sacrifice: Favorite Food
Covenant: Honor Vows

The First Lenten Exercise: Time

- Gather detailed records for the use of time for 1-2 weeks.
- Be specific: lunch, driving, etc.
- Work time is exclusive of transportation and lunch.
- Categorize use of time according to the spreadsheet.
- Absolute certainty is not as important as an accurate view.
- Note variance with balanced orientation.

Time has been given to you by God as a gift. How you spend it is the surest sign of your orientation toward self.

The Basic Principles Regarding Time

- **Toward God:**
  God is called to receive the "first fruits" of the gifts he gives us, which means he gets THE FIRST 2.5 hours of every day.
- **Toward Others:**
  We should spend twice the time with others as we spend alone and triple the time with family as with others.
- **Toward Self:**
  Time is to be spent for re-creation, not indulgence.

The Use of Time

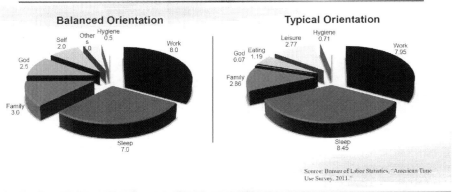

Source: Bureau of Labor Statistics, "American Time Use Survey, 2011."

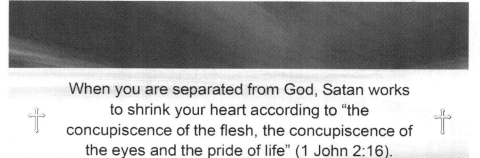

When you are separated from God, Satan works to shrink your heart according to "the concupiscence of the flesh, the concupiscence of the eyes and the pride of life" (1 John 2:16).

Consumption of Pornography

- Pornography consumption has exploded in past generation.
- Magnitude is hidden by several factors including: under reporting of revenue and technological change.
- In late 1950's typical was a stag film costing over $100.
- In mid 1970's typical was a magazine costing $5.
- In late 1980's typical was a rented VHS costing $2.
- Today it is the internet.

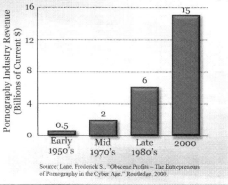

Source: Lane, Frederick S., "Obscene Profits – The Entrepreneurs of Pornography in the Cyber Age," Routledge, 2000.

Pornography in a Man's Brain

- Sexually stimulating images are processed as real at the emotional, not intellectual level.
- The brain focuses on visual stimuli within milliseconds.
- Visual stimuli entering through the eye bypass the neocortex and go directly from the thalamus to the amygdala.
- In less than one second the brain is flooded with a chemical cocktail including: testosterone, oxytocin, vasopressin, epinephrine, nor-epinephrine and dopamine.

The Chemistry of Addiction

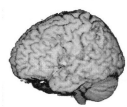

- The individual is led into isolation as the right brain overwhelms the left brain and speech is shut down.
- Testosterone increases mental activity and enables the person to form a more vivid image.
- Vasopressin/Oxytocin bind the person to the object of their desire.
- Dopamine, epinephrine and norepinephrine are addictive stimulants processed like cocaine.
- Lust is addictive.

An Altered Mental Reality

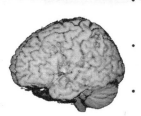

- We learn by creating or changing neurological pathways in the brain, which determine the brain's circuitry.
- Emotional stimuli are imprinted through the amygdala at a much deeper level than rational stimuli are imprinted through the neocortex.
- The more shocking or emotional a stimuli, the deeper it is imprinted.
- Pornographic images viewed for seconds leave imprints that last for years.

Pornography consumption shrinks the heart of a man so that his fatherhood is devalued to the point of a moment of pleasure or worse.

Pornography Devalues Fatherhood

- By age 15, over 90% of males have seen both a Playboy and x-rated film.
- Pornography is consumed as frequently as alcohol on college campuses (>70% monthly).
- Pornography use correlated with promiscuous sex: daily users have 5 times the number of partners as nonusers.
- Pornography acceptance/use correlated to endorsement of cohabitation and out-of-wedlock childbearing.

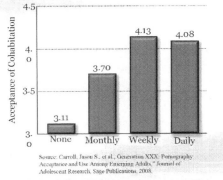

Source: Carroll, Jason S., et al., Generation XXX: Pornography Acceptance and Use Among Emerging Adults," Journal of Adolescent Research, Sage Publications, 2008.

The Objectification of Fatherhood

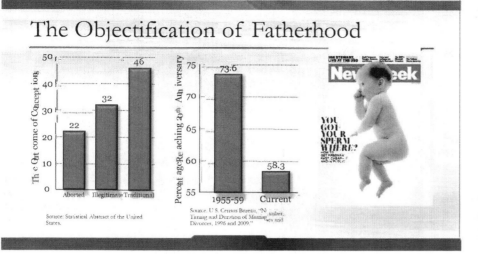

Source: Statistical Abstract of the United States.

Source: U.S. Census Bureau, "Number, Timing and Duration of Marriage Divorces, 1996 and 2009."

The Father who is rich in mercy has the ability to free a heart enslaved by pornography and enlarge it to all that it was created to be.

The Story of Donny Pauling

- Son of a Protestant minister.
- Begins heavy consumption of pornography.
- Becomes a major producer of pornography.
- Specializes in "new talent."
- Shoots over 2 million photographs.
- Films thousands of hours of footage.
- Destroys the life of the women he filmed.
- Offered exclusive contract by Playboy.
- Turns down contract and leaves the pornography industry.
- Documented in "Hope Undimmed: Session 1"

The Seven Steps to Sexual Purity

1. Enter into a relationship with Christ in the Eucharist and ask for the grace to see women as he saw his mother at the foot of the Cross.
2. Remove yourself from temptations against purity.
3. Modify your consumption of alcohol and food.
4. When looking at a woman, focus on her face and transform her into a person by talking about her family.
5. Never publicly speak ill about your spouse or participate in derogatory conversations about women.
6. Whenever you've fallen, go to confession.
7. Seek professional help when you can't stop consumption on your own.

Fulfilling Authentic Male Leadership

Political Leadership Foundation for Future	Moral Leadership Personal Responsibility
Sacrifice The willingness to pay the price.	
Economic Leadership Foundation for Future	Military Leadership Clarity of Thought Integrity of Action

Covenant on Honor of Wedding Vows

"I will honor my wedding vows by living in sexual purity according to the sixth and ninth commandments and I will take whatever action is necessary to safeguard sexual purity for myself, my spouse and my children."

TMIY

Small Group Discussion

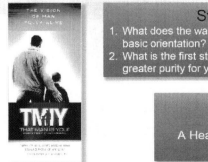

Starter Questions

1. What does the way you spend your time reveal about your basic orientation?
2. What is the first step that you need to take to embrace greater purity for yourself and your family?

Next Week
A Heart Bound by the World

SESSION 19

A Heart Bound by the World

To "become a man after God's own heart" we must not allow our hearts to be shrunk by "the concupiscence of the flesh, the concupiscence of the eyes or the pride of life.

The Daily Lenten Program

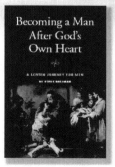

Becoming a Man After God's Own Heart

1. Begin the day with a consecration of the day and ourselves to God.
2. Daily exercise to help us overcome the obstacles in the spiritual life and encounter God.
3. Daily sacrifice designed to coordinate with the daily exercise.
4. Brief examination of conscience at the end of the day.

The Weekly Lenten Program

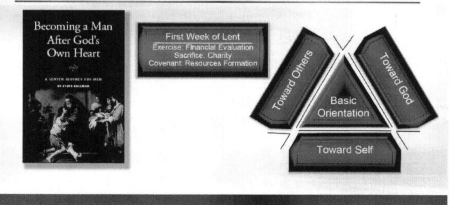

First Week of Lent
Exercise: Financial Evaluation
Sacrifice: Charity
Covenant: Resources Formation

Toward Others

Toward God

Basic Orientation

Toward Self

The Second Lenten Exercise: Finances

- Gather detailed records relating to your expenditures and debt.
- Convert expenditures to a before tax percentage of earnings.
- Include all tax deductible contributions as towards God.
- Include savings and gifts as towards others.
- Calculate debt and debt service on a before tax basis.
- Categorize using worksheet.

Every time that you make or spend a dollar you interact with another person. How you handle your money is a good indicator of your orientation towards the world and other people.

A Balanced Financial Orientation

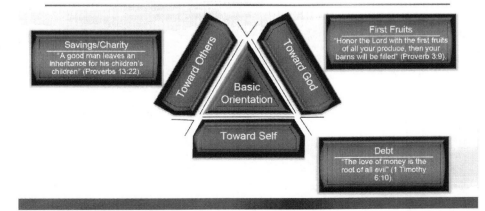

Savings/Charity
"A good man leaves an inheritance for his children's children" (Proverbs 13:22).

Toward Others

Toward God

First Fruits
"Honor the Lord with the first fruits of all your produce, then your barns will be filled" (Proverb 3:9).

Basic Orientation

Toward Self

Debt
"The love of money is the root of all evil" (1 Timothy 6:10).

Consumer Credit

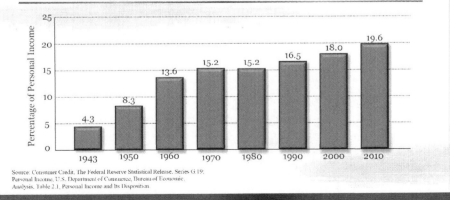

Source: Consumer Credit, The Federal Reserve Statistical Release, Series G.19; Personal Income, U.S. Department of Commerce, Bureau of Economic Analysis, Table 2.1, Personal Income and Its Disposition.

Revolving Credit

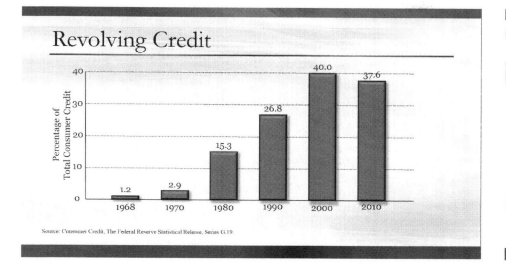

Source: Consumer Credit, The Federal Reserve Statistical Release, Series G.19.

Personal Savings Rate

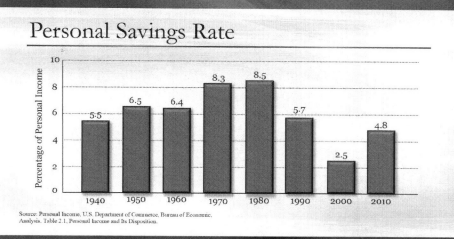

Source: Personal Income, U.S. Department of Commerce, Bureau of Economic, Analysis, Table 2.1, Personal Income and Its Disposition.

Charitable Giving by Individuals

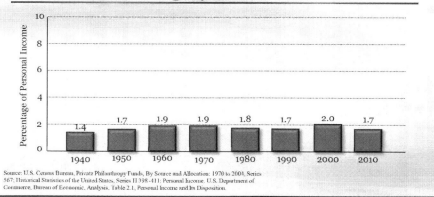

Source: U.S. Census Bureau, Private Philanthropy Funds, By Source and Allocation: 1970 to 2004, Series 567; Historical Statistics of the United States, Series H 398-411; Personal Income, U.S. Department of Commerce, Bureau of Economic, Analysis, Table 2.1, Personal Income and Its Disposition.

Our culture is certainly out of balance when it comes to money. The neurochemistry of our brains can easily get trapped into chasing an illusion.

Addicted to Success

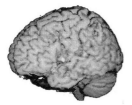

- Testosterone levels increase when we compete. They surge when we win.
- Testosterone relates to increased mental activity, focused attention, increased energy, inexhaustible drive.
- Testosterone enhances the effect of dopamine, which is released when we attain our goal.
- Dopamine is a cocaine like substance that is addictive to the brain.
- After we win, testosterone levels are increased for the next competition.

Net Wealth in America

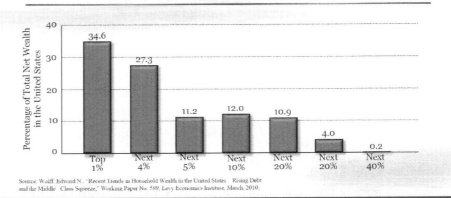

Source: Wolff, Edward N., "Recent Trends in Household Wealth in the United States Rising Debt and the Middle Class Squeeze," Working Paper No. 589, Levy Economics Institute, March, 2010.

Satisfaction in Life

Population Group	Satisfaction
400 Richest Americans (Forbes)	5.8
Pennsylvania Amish	5.8
Inuit people of northern Greenland	5.8
African Maasai	5.7
Swedish probability sample	5.6
International college student sample	4.9
Homeless in Fresno, California	2.9
Calcutta pavement dweller	2.9

Source: Diener, E. and Seligman, M. "Beyond Money – Toward an Economy of Well-Being." Psychological Science in the Public Interest, Volume 5, Number 1, 2004.

The Cost of Financial Stress

Health Issue	Stress	No-Stress	Ratio
Insomnia	39%	17%	2.29
Severe Anxiety	29%	4%	7.25
Migraine	44%	15%	2.93
Severe Depression	23%	4%	5.75
High Blood Pressure	33%	26%	1.27
Heart Arrhythmia	6%	3%	2.00
Ulcers/Digestive Issues	27%	8%	3.38
Back/Muscle Tension	51%	31%	1.65

Source: Associated Press-AOL Health Poll: Credit Card/Debt Stress Study, 2008. See www.hosted.ap.org/specials/interactives/wdc/debt_stress/index.html.

A Very Difficult Truth

"The eye of the covetous man is insatiable in his portion of iniquity: he will not be satisfied till he consume his own soul."

Sirach 14:9

There is a very simple and fundamental reason that we work: to provide for our families. It is essential to our participation in the life of the Father.

An Image of the Providential Father

- "Look at the birds of the air: they neither sow nor reap nor gather into barns, and yet your heavenly Father feeds them" (Matthew 6:26).
- "If any one does not provide for his relatives, and especially for his own family, he has disowned the faith and is worse than an unbeliever" (1 Timothy 5:8).
- One-third of 12-15 year-olds say parental work obligations are the main reason families do not spend time together.
- Parents working late is the #1 reason families do not eat dinner together.

Source: Fatherhood Facts, 4th Edition, National Fatherhood Initiative, 2002.
The Importance of Family Dinners III, CASA, September 2006.

E. Riley Leggett and Another Path

- Born in small East Texas farming community.
- Lived through Great Depression: "I know what it's like to hoe a row of cotton in the Texas heat."
- Stayed home from WWII to care for parents.
- Worked through college.
- Landed in Houston without a nickel to his name.
- "If you ever go to bed hungry just once, it will change you forever. Vowed not one of my kids would go to bed hungry."
- Started two light manufacturing companies.
- "All I ever wanted to be was a father and now all I do is work. From now on we lock the doors at 5:30pm and go have dinner with our families."

The Seven Steps to Financial Freedom

1. Give the first fruits of your labor to God.
2. Moderate your consumption of the media.
3. Cut up all credit cards until they are paid off.
4. Begin saving and gradually increase amount.
5. Live below your means.
6. Cut entertainment expense by eating meals together at home and enjoying nature as recreation.
7. Keep $8 in your wallet that you MUST give away.

Covenant on Resources for Formation

"I will use the fruit of my labor for the formation of others by giving God the first fruits, eliminating all credit card debt and saving for an inheritance for my children's children."

TMIY

Small Group Discussion

Starter Questions

1. What does your financial analysis reveal about your focus on laying a foundation for the future?
2. What is the most important step that you need to take to fulfill the Covenant on Using Money for Formation?

Next Week
A Descent into the Isolation of Self

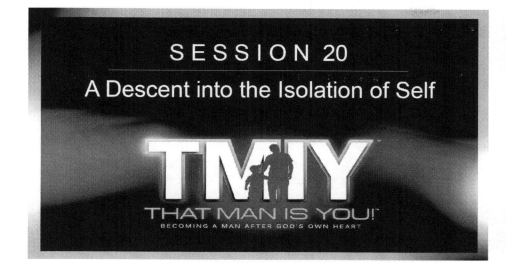

SESSION 20

A Descent into the Isolation of Self

To "become a man after God's own heart" we must not allow our hearts to be shrunk by "the concupiscence of the flesh, the concupiscence of the eyes or the pride of life.

The Daily Lenten Program

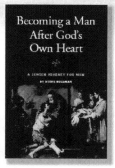

1. Begin the day with a consecration of the day and ourselves to God.
2. Daily exercise to help us overcome the obstacles in the spiritual life and encounter God.
3. Daily sacrifice designed to coordinate with the daily exercise.
4. Brief examination of conscience at the end of the day.

The Weekly Lenten Program

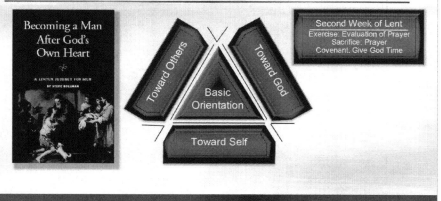

The Third Lenten Exercise: Prayer

- Gather detailed records relating to prayer and spiritual activities.
- Categorize prayer and spiritual activities according to the three fundamental orientations using the provided worksheet.
- Note variance of total time spent in prayer and spiritual exercises.
- Note variance of time spent in prayer and spiritual exercises according to the three fundamental orientations.

Man's union with God elevates man into a life of communion. Satan seeks to separate man from God to plunge him into the abyss of self.

The Plan of God: Joy in Communion

- **Draw Man out of Self:**
  "Through this 'test,' man gains the consciousness of his superiority [and] ... go[es] in some way outside of his own being" (Pope John Paul II, October 10, 1979).
- **Establish Communion with God:**
  "I thirst" (John 19:28).
- **Establish Communion with Others:**
  "Therefore a man leaves his father and his mother and cleaves to his wife, and they become one flesh" (Genesis 2:24).

The Devil's Plan: The Isolation of Self

- **Turn Man in upon Himself:**
  "You will be like God" (Genesis 3:5).
- **Break Communion with God:**
  "When they heard the voice of the Lord God walking in paradise at the afternoon air, they hid themselves from the face of the Lord God" (Genesis 3:7).
- **Break Communion with Others:**
  "When they perceived themselves to be naked, they sewed together fig leaves, and made themselves clothes" (Genesis 3:7).

Let us consider some data to see which of these two plans is being followed today. Let us consider the consequences.

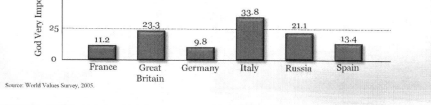

"You will be like God"

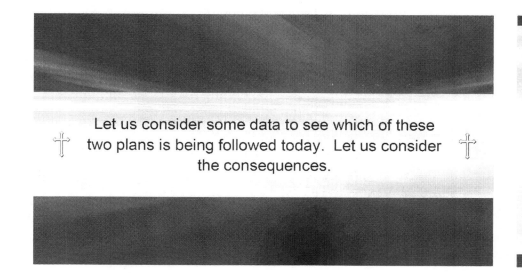

Source: World Values Survey, 2005.

The Descent of the Mind

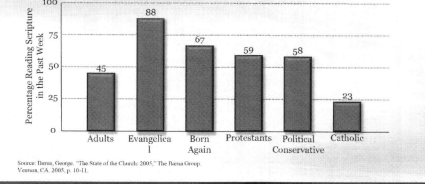

Source: Barna, George. "The State of the Church: 2005," The Barna Group. Ventura, CA. 2005, p. 10-11.

Separation from God

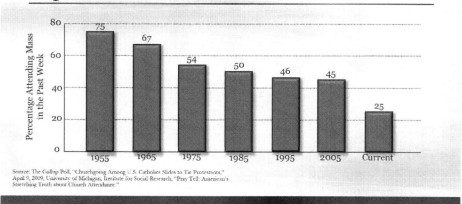

Source: The Gallup Poll, "Churchgoing Among U.S. Catholics Slides to Tie Protestants," April 9, 2009; University of Michigan, Institute for Social Research, "Pray Tell: American's Stretching Truth about Church Attendance."

Separation from Spouse

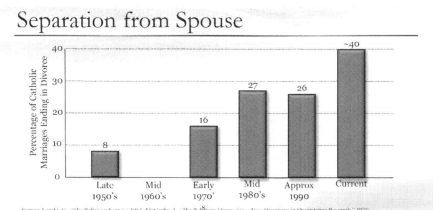

Percentage of Catholic Marriages Ending in Divorce

Late 1950's	8
Mid 1960's	
Early 1970'	16
Mid 1980's	27
Approx 1990	26
Current	~40

Source: Lenski, G., "The Religious Factor," 1961; McCarthy, J., "The Religious Dimension – New Directions in Quantitative Research," 1979; Bumpass, L., Demography, 1990, pp. 484-498., U.S. Census Bureau, "Number, Timing and Duration of Marriages and Divorces, 2009."

It is not Good for Man to be Alone

Death Rate/100,000	Married	Divorced	Ratio
Heart Disease	176	362	2.06
Vehicular Accidents	35	128	3.66
Lung Cancer	28	65	2.32
Digestive Cancer	27	48	1.78
Stroke	24	58	2.42
Suicide	17	73	4.29
Cirrhosis of the Liver	11	79	7.18
Hypertension	8	20	2.50

Source: Lynch, James J., "A Cry Unheard – New Insights into the Medical Consequences of Loneliness," Bancroft Press, 2000, p. 101 Data are for White Males Aged 15-64 from 1959-1961.

The "pride of life" eventually shrinks the human heart until a person is plunged into the isolation of self. An encounter with the Father who is rich in mercy pulls a person back into communion.

The Story of Alexis Carrel

- 1873: Born to devout parents in Lyon, France.
- 1889: Bachelor of Letters, Lyon University.
- 1890: Bachelor of Science, Lyon University.
- 1900: Doctor of Medicine, Lyon University.
- 1889-1900: Becomes a practical atheist while pursuing academic degrees.
- 1902: Publishes work on suture of blood vessels.
- 1912: Awarded Nobel Prize in Medicine.
- 1944: Dies on November 5th.

The Story of Alexis Carrel

- Boards train to Lourdes on May 25, 1902.
- Marie Bailly, at the point of death from tubercular peritonitis, is secretly placed on the train.
- In route, Dr. Carrel correctly diagnoses Marie Bailly and states she will die before arriving in Lourdes.
- Marie Bailly is taken to baths.
- An instantaneous cure occurs when water is poured over her stomach.
- Dr. Carrel takes notes so feverously that he begins writing on his shirt sleeve.

"Gentle Virgin, who bringeth help to the unfortunate who humbly implore thee. Keep me with thee. I believe in thee. Thou didst answer my prayers by a blazing miracle. I am still blind to it. I still doubt. But the greatest desire of my life, my highest aspiration, is to believe, to believe passionately, implicitly, and never more to analyze and doubt. Thy name is more gracious than the morning sun. Take unto thyself this uneasy sinner with the anxious frown and troubled heart who has exhausted himself in the vain pursuit of fantasies. Beneath the deep, harsh warnings of my intellectual pride a smothered dream persists. Alas, it is still only a dream, but the most enchanting of them all. It is the dream of believing in thee and of loving thee with the shining spirit of the men of God."

The Story of Alexis Carrel

- Struggles to accept faith for the next 42 years.
- Reports "inexplicable cure" and is rejected by French academia. Moves to the United States.
- 1910: Witnesses 2nd instantaneous cure of a 18 month old child born blind. Marries nurse.
- 1935: Writes "Man, the Unknown" and embraces mystical view of nature and concept of eugenics.
- Writings are used by Nazis to support their T-4 euthanasia program.
- WWII: French Foundation for the Study of Human Problems.

The Story of Alexis Carrel

- 1938: Meets Dom Alexis Presse
- 1942: "I believe in the existence of God, in the immortality of the soul, in Revelation and in all that the Catholic Church teaches."
- "When one approaches one's own death, one grasps the nothingness of all things. I have gained fame. The world speaks of me and of my works, yet I am a mere child before God, and a poor child at that."
- 1945: Dies on November 5th.

We must become men of prayer. We must learn to give God some of our time so that he may expand our heart to all that it was created to be.

Covenant on Giving Time to God

"I will give some of my time to God, beginning with Sunday, the Lord's Day. I will attend Mass together with my family and make the gift of that day to my family so that we may experience the superabundant joy of God together."

TMIY

Small Group Discussion

Starter Questions
1. What does your prayer life reveal about your clarity of thought and integrity of action?
2. What is best prayer that you've ever uttered to God?

Next Week
The Ascent of the Mind to God

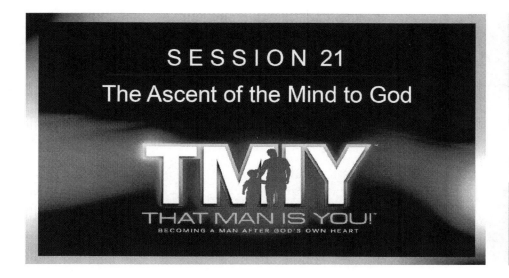

SESSION 21

The Ascent of the Mind to God

TMIY
THAT MAN IS YOU!
BECOMING A MAN AFTER GOD'S OWN HEART

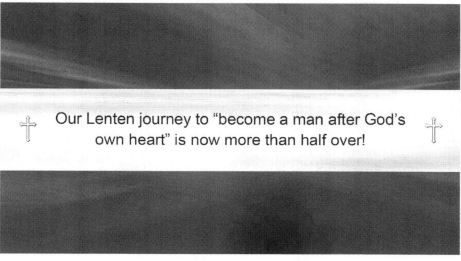

✝ Our Lenten journey to "become a man after God's own heart" is now more than half over! ✝

The Daily Lenten Program

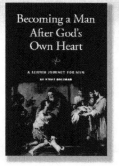

Becoming a Man After God's Own Heart

A LENTEN JOURNEY FOR MEN
BY STEVE BOLLMAN

1. Begin the day with a consecration of the day and ourselves to God.
2. Daily exercise to help us overcome the obstacles in the spiritual life and encounter God.
3. Daily sacrifice designed to coordinate with the daily exercise.
4. Brief examination of conscience at the end of the day.

The Weekly Lenten Program

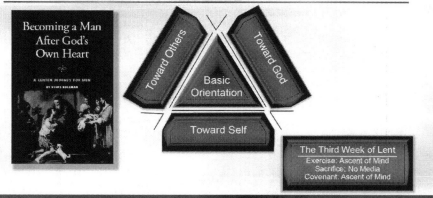

Becoming a Man After God's Own Heart

A LENTEN JOURNEY FOR MEN
BY STEVE BOLLMAN

Toward Others
Toward God
Basic Orientation
Toward Self

The Third Week of Lent
Exercise: Ascent of Mind
Sacrifice: No Media
Covenant: Ascent of Mind

Satan is constantly trying to shrink your heart. To get you to believe that you are less than you truly are. But the human person is truly awesome.

The Wonder of the Human Person

- One thousand, million, million, million, million atoms combined into 75 trillion cells.
- One billion neurons, stretching over one million miles, processing 38 thousand trillions bits per second.
- 120 million rod cells and 6 million cone cells sending information down 1.2 million nerve fibers.
- 20,000 hair cells sensitive to one billionth of an atmospheric pressure.
- 100,000 heart beats, pumping 2000 gallons of blood through 60,000 miles of blood vessels every day.
- 700 million alveoli containing 300,000 million capillaries, breathing 29,000 times per day.

The Challenge for Modern Man

" The first swallow from the cup of natural sciences makes atheists, but at the bottom of the cup God is waiting. "

Werner Heisenberg
Nobel Laureate, Physics, 1932

Dr. Gerald Schroeder

- Bachelor, Master and Doctorate in Nuclear Physics from M.I.T.
- Present at the detonation of 6 atomic bombs.
- Author of over 60 professional articles.
- Patent holder for the first real time monitor of airborne alpha, beta, gamma emitters.
- "I am called to be a philosopher of nuclear physics!"
- Author of Genesis and the Big Bang, The Science of God, The Hidden Face of God and God According to God.

The Science of God

- Considers Biblical text for the creation of the world found in Genesis Chapter 1.
- Considers ancient Jewish commentary on the creation of the world.
- Considers science of modern cosmology.
- Uses Einstein's Theory of Relativity to reconcile.
- "Both stories are true. It just depends on the time-spaces coordinates one uses for a reference point. Genesis is God standing at the Big Bang looking forward. Cosmology is man standing on earth looking backwards."

Creation: Genesis and Cosmology

Biblical Account	Time Billions of years BP	Modern Cosmology
Day 1: "Let there be light."	15.75 – 7.75	Big Bang, Light, Galaxies form.
Day 2: "Let there be a firmament."	7.75 – 3.75	Milky Way Galaxy and Sun form.
Day 3: "Let dry land appear."	3.75 – 1.75	Formation of Water, Bacteria, Algae
Day 4: "Let there be lights in heaven."	1.75 – 0.75	Photosynthesis, Transparent Atmosphere.
Day 5: "Let water have life/birds."	0.75 – 0.25	Cambrian explosion of life, winged insects.
Day 6: "Let land have life/humanity."	0.25 – Now	Land animals, extinction, humans.
Day 7: "God rested."	Present	Life as we know it.

Source: Schroeder, Gerald L., "The Science of God – The Convergence of Science and Biblical Wisdom," The Free Press, 1997, p. 67.

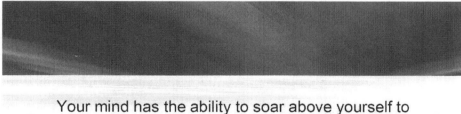

Your mind has the ability to soar above yourself to touch God. He has given you the perfect means: the Bible.

The Lamp to Enlighten our Minds

- "Thy word is a lamp to my feet and a light to my path" (Psalm 119:105).
- "Let [the faithful] remember, however, that prayer should accompany the reading of Sacred Scripture, so that a dialogue takes place between God and man. For 'we speak to him when we pray; we listen to him when we read the divine oracles'" (Catechism #2653).
- There are four elements to Lectio Divina: Reading, Meditation, Prayer and Contemplation.

Lectio or Reading

- Place the Word of God on your lips.
- Gently read a passage from the Bible.
- When a thought, word or line strikes you, stop and dwell on that text, repeating it slowly over and over.
- When the passage has "dried up," move on to the next passage.

Meditatio or Meditation

- Dwelling at leisure on a morsel of text.
- Personalize passage: "What is God saying to ME through the passage?"
- Do not work hard to actively try to "crack" the text.
- Listen so that the text might speak.
- Let God speak through the text.

Oratio or Prayer

- The Word moves from the lips to the heart.
- Desire for the text to be "opened up."
- "Lord, that I might see!"
- It is personalized.
- It is ultimately desire for communion with God.

Contemplatio or Contemplation

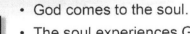

- God comes to the soul.
- The soul experiences God's love being poured into it.
- This is God's initiative to be received by the soul as "gift."
- The soul is passive and receives or "lingers" as long as God's presence is experienced.

A Word of Caution

- Our fallen nature is still active.
- We are capable of projecting our own desires into the Scriptures.
- We must read Scripture with the mind of the Church.
- There is only "one voice" of God.
- What we "hear" from God through the Scriptures must be in harmony with the "voice of God" speaking through the Church on teachings of faith and morals.

✝ God will speak to you personally through the Scriptures. It might just change your life! ✝

St. Augustine

354: Born Nov. 13th in North Africa.

Youth: Receives Christian education.

370: Goes to Carthage to further education.

372: Has an illegitimate son.

373: Embraces the heresy Manichaeism.

383: Goes to Rome and then Milan.

386: Is converted in garden.

387: Baptized by St. Ambrose in Milan.

391: Ordained a priest.

396: Ordained bishop of Hippo in Africa.

430: Dies on August 28th.

The Wanderings of St. Augustine

"So for the space of nine years (from my nineteenth to my twenty-eighth year) I lived a life in which I was seduced and seducing, deceived and deceiving, the prey of various desires. My public life was that of a teacher of what are called the 'liberal arts.' In private I went under cover of a false kind of religion. I was arrogant in the one sphere, superstitious in the other, and vain and empty from all points of view" (Confessions, Book IV, Chapter 1).

The Conversion of St. Augustine

"A huge storm rose up within me ... Suddenly, a voice reaches my ears from a nearby house ... 'Take it and read it' ... I snatched up the book, opened it, and read in silence the passage upon which my eyes first fell: 'Not in rioting and drunkenness, not in chambering and wantonness, not is strife and envying; but put ye on the Lord Jesus Christ, and make not provision for the flesh in concupiscence.' I had no wish to read further; there was no need to" (Confessions, Book VIII, Chapter 12).

The Heart of St. Augustine

- "O Lord, you have made us for yourself, and our hearts are restless until they rest in thee" (Confessions, Book 1, Chapter 1).

- "Late have I loved thee, beauty ever ancient, ever new, late have I loved thee! You were within me and I was outside, and there I sought for you and in my ugliness I plunged into the beauties that you have made. You were with me, and I was not with you ... You called, you cried out, you shattered my deafness: you flashed, you shone, you scattered my blindness: you breathed perfume, and I drew in my breath and I pant for you: I tasted, and I am hungry and thirsty ... When in my whole self I shall cling to you united, I shall find no sorrow anywhere, no labor; wholly alive will my life be all full of you" (Confessions, Book X, Chapters 27-28).

Covenant on the Ascent of Mind to God

"I will elevate my mind to God by spending at least fifteen minutes each day gently reading Scripture and allowing God to speak to me. I will validate my insights through my spouse and/or spiritual guide as appropriate."

TMIY

Small Group Discussion

Starter Questions
1. When has God personally guided your life through the Scriptures?
2. When will you set aside 15 minutes to read Scripture each day? Will you do so with your spouse?

Next Week
The Practice of the Presence of God

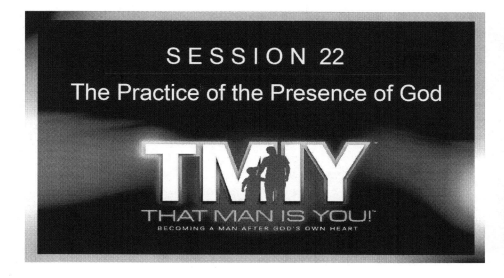

SESSION 22

The Practice of the Presence of God

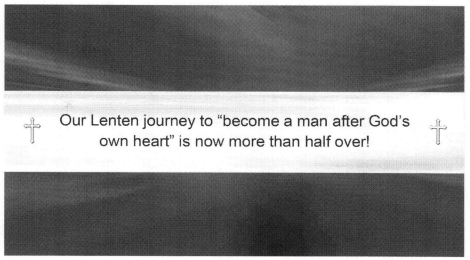

Our Lenten journey to "become a man after God's own heart" is now more than half over!

The Daily Lenten Program

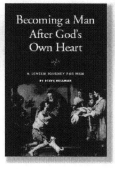

Becoming a Man After God's Own Heart

A LENTEN JOURNEY FOR MEN

1. Begin the day with a consecration of the day and ourselves to God.
2. Daily exercise to help us overcome the obstacles in the spiritual life and encounter God.
3. Daily sacrifice designed to coordinate with the daily exercise.
4. Brief examination of conscience at the end of the day.

The Weekly Lenten Program

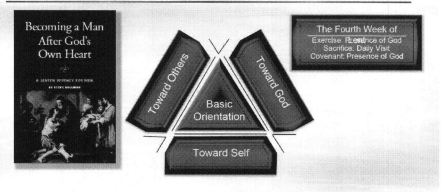

The Fourth Week of
Exercise: Presence of God
Sacrifice: Daily Visit
Covenant: Presence of God

Last week, we discovered that the true desires of the human heart transcend this world and can only be fulfilled by God.

The Desire of the Human Heart

- "O Lord, you have made us for yourself, and our hearts are restless until they rest in thee" (Confessions, Book 1, Chapter 1).
- "Late have I loved thee, beauty ever ancient, ever new, late have I loved thee! You were within me and I was outside, and there I sought for you and in my ugliness I plunged into the beauties that you have made. You were with me, and I was not with you ... You called, you cried out, you shattered my deafness: you flashed, you shone, you scattered my blindness: you breathed perfume, and I drew in my breath and I pant for you: I tasted, and I am hungry and thirsty" (Confessions, Book X, Chapters 27-28).

The Desire of the "Heart" of God

- "Thus says the high and lofty One who inhabits eternity, whose name is Holy, 'I dwell in the high and holy place, and also with him who is of a contrite and humble spirit" (Isaiah 57:15).
- "If a man loves me, he will keep my word, and my Father will love him, and we will come to him and make our home with him" (John 14:23).

Man desires God. God desires man. These desires are called to meet and to be fulfilled in the human heart.

The Thirst of Jesus Christ

- "After this Jesus, knowing that all was now finished, said (to fulfill the Scripture), 'I thirst'" (John 19:28).
- "But one of the soldiers pierced his side with a spear, and at once there came out blood and water … For these things took place that the Scripture might be fulfilled" (John 19:34-36).
- Beloved, do not pass over this mystery without thought … I said that the water and blood symbolized baptism and the holy Eucharist. From these two sacraments the Church is born … Do you understand … what food he gives us all to eat" (St. John Chrysostom, Office of Readings, Good Friday)?

The Mystery of the Eucharist

"Jesus said to them, 'I am the bread of life; he who comes to me shall not hunger, and he who believes in me shall never thirst' … the Jews then murmured at him, because he said, 'I am the bread of life.'"

John 6:35-41

The Mystery of the Eucharist

"[Jesus said], 'Truly, truly, I am the bread of life … I am the living bread which came down from heaven; if any one eats of this bread, he will live for ever; and the bread which I shall give for the life of the world is my flesh' … The Jews then disputed among themselves, saying, 'How can this man give us his flesh to eat?'"

John 6:51-52

The Mystery of the Eucharist

"Jesus said to them, 'Truly, truly, I say to you, unless you eat the flesh of the Son of man and drink his blood, you have no life in you … for my flesh is food indeed, and my blood is drink indeed. He who eats my flesh and drinks my blood abides in me and I in him' … Many of his disciples said, 'This is a hard saying; who can listen to it?'"

John 6:53-60

The Mystery of the Eucharist

"Jesus, knowing in himself that his disciples murmured at it, said to them, 'Do you take offense at this? What if you were to see the Son of man ascending where he was before?' ... After this many of his disciples drew back and no longer went about with him ... Simon Peter said, 'Lord, to whom shall we go? You have the words of eternal life.'"

John 6:61-68

How few of us grasp what Christ wishes to do for our hearts. He has given us the first saint of the new millennium to be our guide.

The Life of St. Faustina Kowalska

- 1905: Born in Lodz, Poland.
- 1912: Receives God's call, which she resists.
- 1923: Christ appears to her while she's dancing: "How long shall I put up with you and how long will you keep putting me off?"
- 1925: Enters convent.
- 1931: Vision of Divine Mercy of Christ. Has almost daily visions and conversations with Christ for the next 7 years.
- 1935: Receives the Divine Mercy Chaplet.
- 1938: Dies on October 5th.
- 2000: Canonized as the first saint of the new millennium on April 16th.

Christ's Life in the Soul

"How very much I desire the salvation of souls! My dearest secretary, write that I want to pour out My divine life into human souls and to sanctify them, if only they were willing to accept My grace. The greatest sinners would achieve great sanctity, if only they would trust in My mercy ... My kingdom on earth is My life in the human soul."

Divine Mercy in My Soul, #1784

Christ's Life in the Soul

"My daughter, even though you do not perceive Me in the most secret depths of your heart, you still cannot say that I am not there. I only remove from you the awareness of My presence … to achieve My unfathomable ends, which you will know of later on."

Divine Mercy in My Soul, #1181

Christ as the King of Mercy

- "Before I come as the just Judge, I am coming first as the King of Mercy" (Divine Mercy in My Soul, #83).
- "God sent the Son into the world, not to condemn the world, but that the world might be saved through him" (John 3:17).
- "If you continue in my word … the truth will make you free" (John 8:31-32).
- "I came that they may have life, and have it abundantly" (John 10:10).
- "These things I have spoken to you, that my joy may be in you, and that your joy may be full" (John 15:11).

- "I am always in your heart; not only when you receive Me in Holy Communion, but always" (Divine Mercy in My Soul, #575).
- We must learn to extend this moment throughout our lives.

The Practice of the Presence of God

"I cannot express to you what is taking place in me at present … I devote myself exclusively to remaining always in his holy presence. I keep myself in his presence by simple attentiveness and a general loving awareness of God that I call 'actual presence of God' or better, a quiet and secret conversation of the soul with God that is lasting."

Brother Lawrence

The Practice of the Presence of God

> I derive greater sweetness and satisfaction than an infant receives from his mother's breast. Therefore, if I may dare use the expression, I would gladly call this state the 'breasts of God,' because of the indescribable sweetness I taste and experience there … This sometimes results in interior, and often exterior, contentment and joys so great that I have to perform childish acts to control them and keep them from showing outwardly.
>
> Brother Lawrence

Practical Advice on the Presence of God

1. At Mass
- Arrive early. Silently pray after Mass.
- "My Lord and my God."

2. At Home
- Holy Water dish at major entrances.
- Enter: "I rejoiced when I heard them say, 'Let us got to the house of the Lord.'"
- Exit: "One day within your house is better than a thousand elsewhere."

3. Throughout the Day
- Find something repetitive in your schedule and use it as a trigger to unite yourself to God.

Covenant on the Practice of the Presence of God

"I will Practice the Presence of God by receiving Christ in the Eucharist one day each week in addition to Sunday. If I am unable to receive Him in the Eucharist, I will at least stop to visit Him residing in the Tabernacle."

TMIY

Small Group Discussion

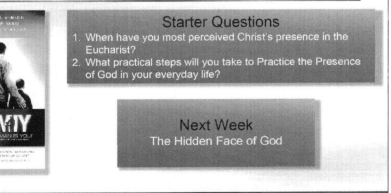

Starter Questions
1. When have you most perceived Christ's presence in the Eucharist?
2. What practical steps will you take to Practice the Presence of God in your everyday life?

Next Week
The Hidden Face of God

SESSION 23

The Hidden Face of God

✝ Our Lenten journey to "become a man after God's own heart" speeds to its conclusion. You still have time for a novena. ✝

The Daily Lenten Program

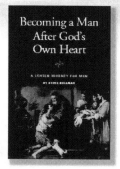

1. Begin the day with a consecration of the day and ourselves to God.
2. Daily exercise to help us overcome the obstacles in the spiritual life and encounter God.
3. Daily sacrifice designed to coordinate with the daily exercise.
4. Brief examination of conscience at the end of the day.

The Weekly Lenten Program

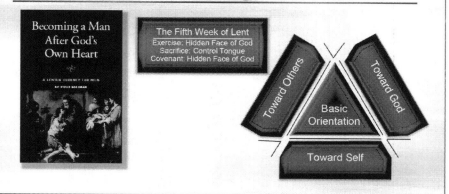

The Fifth Week of Lent
Exercise: Hidden Face of God
Sacrifice: Control Tongue
Covenant: Hidden Face of God

Toward Others
Toward God
Basic Orientation
Toward Self

Last week we had to expand our heart to create a dwelling place for God. This week we must expand it still larger so that it can embrace God dwelling in another person.

The Devil's Plan: Strife Leading to Death

- **The Garden of Eden:**
  "Your desire shall be for your husband, and he shall rule over you ... you are dust, and to dust you shall return" (Genesis 3:16-19).
- **The Survival of the Fittest:**
  "As many more individuals of each species are born that can possibly survive ... there is a frequently recurring struggle for existence" (Charles Darwin, The Origin of Species, Introduction).
- **The Constant State of War:**
  "During the time men live without a common power to keep them all in awe, they are in that condition called war ... every man against every man ... No arts; no letters; no society; and which is worst of all, continual fear, and danger of violent death; and the life of man, solitary, poor, nasty, brutish and short" (Thomas Hobbes, Leviathan, Chapter 12).

The Plan of God: God is in Communion

"Man became the image of God not only through his own humanity, but also through the communion of persons, which man and woman form from the very beginning ... Man becomes the image of God not so much in the moment of solitude as in the moment of communion."

Pope John Paul II
November 14, 1979

Last week we saw that through the Eucharist, Christ profoundly dwells in our souls. Through the Eucharist, Christ also dwells in other souls.

The Story of St. Anthony Marie Claret

- 1807: Born near Barcelona, Spain.
- 1835: Ordained to priesthood.
- 1848: Missionary to Canary Islands.
- 1849: Founds Missionary Sons of the Immaculate Heart of Mary (Claretians).
- 1849: Appointed Archbishop of Santiago, Cuba.
- 1857: Confessor to Queen Isabella II of Spain.
- 1869: Participated in Vatican I.
- 1870: Died on October 24 in southern France.

A Living Tabernacle

"On August 26, 1861, finding myself at prayer in the church of the Holy Rosary, at La Branja, at seven o'clock in the evening, the Lord granted me the grace of conserving the Sacramental Species within my heart … I now bear within me day and night the adorable Eucharist. I must therefore be always recollected and cultivate the interior life."

St. Anthony Marie Claret

An Important Lesson

- St. Philip Neri observed a man leaving church immediately after receiving Communion.
- He called two acolytes and had them follow the man with lighted candles.
- The man returned to St. Philip Neri to ask why he had done such a thing.
- St. Philip Neri replied: "It is to pay proper respect to Our Lord, whom you are carrying away with you. Since you neglect to adore Him, I sent servers to take your place."

Our Lady as a Living Tabernacle

"Mary arose and went with haste into the hill country … and she entered the house of Zechariah and greeted Elizabeth. And when Elizabeth heard the greeting of Mary, the babe leaped in her womb; and Elizabeth was filled with the Holy Spirit and she exclaimed with a loud cry, 'Blessed are you among women, and blessed is the fruit of your womb' … For behold, when the voice of your greeting came to my ears, the babe in my womb leaped for joy."

Luke 1:39-44

- Christ's presence in the soul is not restricted to the Eucharistic encounter.
- "By His incarnation the Son of God has united Himself in some fashion with every man" (*Gaudium et Spes*, #22).

The Story of John Pridmore

- Born in 1964 in London.
- Age 11: After his parents divorce, made the unconscious decision to no longer love.
- Age 14: Started stealing.
- Age 15: Placed in a youth detention center.
- Age 19: Placed in an adult prison.
- Age 20: Entered London's underworld, working as an enforcer in the mafia and dealing drugs.
- Age 27: Left a man for dead outside a pub.
- Age 44: Spoke to 400,000 youth at World Youth Day in Sydney, Australia.

The Descent of John Pridmore

- By mid 20's, he lives a life of rage.
- After getting stabbed in a bar, takes revenge by pounding the man's head against the cement in full view of his son and elementary students.
- Destroys pubs and people with pool cues.
- Leaves a man for dead because he refused to drink his pint quickly enough.
- "Jesus loves you."
- Mother: "I've prayed for you every day of your life. But two weeks ago … I prayed to Jesus to take you. If it meant you dying, then to let you die, but not to let you hurt yourself or anyone else any more."

The Conversion of John Pridmore

- Has money, girls and the "respect" of the underworld.
- Realizes that he isn't happy and the drugs are making him paranoid.
- Opens Bible and reads the story of the Prodigal Son. Breaks down crying and is converted.
- Receives "permission" to leave the mafia: "It's my insurance in case there is a God."
- Gives a holy card to his "father" in the mafia, who prays it every night before bed.
- Preaches at the death of his "father" in the mafia.

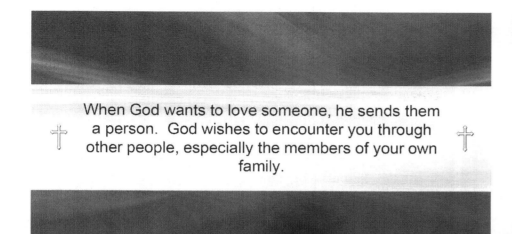

When God wants to love someone, he sends them a person. God wishes to encounter you through other people, especially the members of your own family.

Encountering God in the Poor

- "Truly, I say to you, as you did it to one of the least of my brethren, you did it to me" (Matthew 25:40).
- "They are Jesus. Each one is Jesus in a distressing disguise" (Mother Teresa).

Encountering God in your Home

- "Where two or three are gathered in my name, there am I in the midst of them" (Matthew 18:20).
- "Shelly receive this ring as a sign of my love and fidelity. In the name of the Father, and of the Son and of the Holy Spirit" (Marriage Ceremony).
- "Whoever receives one such child in my name receives me" (Matthew 18:).

The Practice of the Hidden Face of God

1. God dwells in the midst of your spousal union by definition.
2. God dwells in your children by definition.
3. Each time that your spouse and/or children walk up to you, God is walking up to you in them.
4. Let your spouse and children become for you the Hidden Face of God.
5. "Speak Lord, for your servant is listening" (1 Samuel 3:10).
6. "Lord, show me your face. Let your voice sound in my ears; for your voice is sweet and your face comely" (Song of Solomon 2:14).
7. Offer God a "sacrifice of praise" 7 times each day for finding his Hidden Face in your spouse and children.

The Story of Dom Bellorger

- Veterinarian by trade.
- Meets a Trappist brother on a train and goes to a Trappist monastery where he experiences a radical conversion.
- Becomes a Trappist monk.
- Awakes to the fact that he has joined a group of "tired farmers."
- Appointed Abbott of community.
- Privately asks each monk to adore 7 times/day.
- The monastery is transformed within six months.

Covenant on the Hidden Face of God

"I will stop what I am doing and praise God seven times each day for discovering his Hidden Face in those closest to me, especially my wife and children."

TMIY

Small Group Discussion

Starter Questions
1. When have you most profoundly seen God manifest in your spouse or children?
2. What is the greatest obstacle that prevents you from perceiving Christ's Hidden Face in other people?

Next Week
The Triumph of Mercy

SESSION 24

The Triumph of Mercy

This is Holy Week. We must follow Christ until the end if we wish our Lenten journey "to become a man after God's own heart" to bear fruit.

The Daily Lenten Program

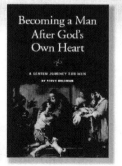

1. Begin the day with a consecration of the day and ourselves to God.
2. Daily exercise to help us overcome the obstacles in the spiritual life and encounter God.
3. Daily sacrifice designed to coordinate with the daily exercise.
4. Brief examination of conscience at the end of the day.

The Weekly Lenten Program

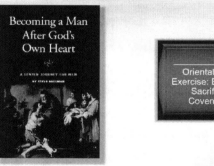

Holy Week

Orientation: The Merciful Father
Exercise: Examination of Conscience
Sacrifice: Miserere of David
Covenant: The Mercy of God

Enlarging the Human Heart

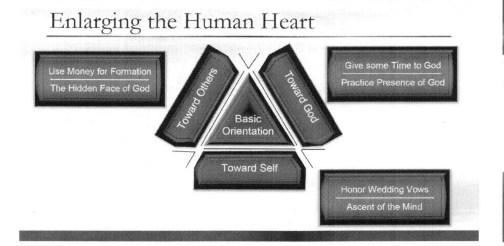

- Use Money for Formation
- The Hidden Face of God
- Toward Others
- Toward God
- Give some Time to God
- Practice Presence of God
- Basic Orientation
- Toward Self
- Honor Wedding Vows
- Ascent of the Mind

King David became a "man after God's own heart" not because he was innocent of sin, but because having sinned, he encountered the Father, rich in mercy, and allowed him to expand his heart to all that it was created to be.

The Descent of King David

- Commits adultery with Bathsheba, who becomes pregnant with his child.
- Arranges for the death of Bathsheba's husband, Uriah.
- "Do not let this matter trouble you, for the sword devours now one and now another."
- Takes Bathsheba for his wife.
- Confronted by the Prophet Nathan who tells David the parable of the two men.
- "David said to Nathan, 'I have sinned against the Lord.'"

The Repentance of King David

Have mercy on me, O God according to thy steadfast love; according to thy abundant mercy blot out my transgressions … Against thee, thee only, have I sinned, and done that which is evil in thy sight, so that thou art justified in thy sentence and blameless in thy judgment … Create in me a clean heart, O God, and put a new and right spirit within me. Cast me not away from thy presence … O Lord, open thou my lips, and my mouth shall show forth thy praise. For thou hast no delight in sacrifice … The sacrifice acceptable to God is a broken spirit; a broken and contrite heart, O God, thou wilt not despise."

Psalm 51:1-17

King David's repentance transformed him into "a man after God's own heart." The power of repentance is almost beyond our comprehension.

The Story of St. John Bosco

- 1815: Born August 16th in Turin, Italy.
- 1824: Dream at age 9 reveals life's vocation.
- 1841: Ordained to priesthood. Begins Oratory modeled on father in family on December 8th.
- 1846: Almost dies.
- 1847: Takes in first boarder.
- 1859: Founds Salesians (2nd largest order).
- 1888: Dies on January 31st.
- 1934: Canonized – "The supernatural and miraculous became ordinary."

The Dream of St. John Bosco

- In a field full of boys – some fighting and using bad language.
- Don Bosco loses temper, runs in and begins "laying about with his fists."
- "A noble man" appears telling him that he must teach them through kindness to be good and avoid evil.
- Don Bosco demands: "Who are you to tell me to do these difficult things?"
- "The son of the woman your mother taught you to salute three times a day. If you follow her, these things will be easy."
- Our Lady appears and transforms the rough boys into lambs.

The Power of a Good Confession

- Boy from Oratory (Charles) dead 12 hours.
- Prior to death he called for Don Bosco to hear his confession, but he was out of town.
- Don Bosco arrives and dismisses mourners except mother and aunt: "Charles, rise."
- "Don Bosco! I called for you … It's a wonder I'm not in hell. In my last confession, I didn't dare confess a sin."
- Confession is made. Charles talks with relatives for 2 hours.
- "You are in a state of grace. Heaven stands open to you. Do you want to go to heaven or remain with us?"
- Charles bids his family farewell, lays down and closes his eyes for good.

The Four Elements of a Good Confession

1. Examination of Conscience

2. Contrition

3. Confession

4. Satisfaction

Examination of Conscience

The reception of this sacrament ought to be prepared for by an examination of conscience made in light of the Word of God. The passages best suited to this can be found in the moral catechesis of the Gospels and the apostolic Letters, such as the Sermon on the Mount and the apostolic teachings.

Catechism #1454

Contrition

Among the penitent's acts, contrition occupies first place. Contrition is 'sorrow of the soul and detestation for the sin committed, together with the resolution not to sin again.'

Catechism #1451

Confession

The confession (or disclosure) of sins, even from a simply human point of view, frees us and facilitates our reconciliation with others ... Confession to a priest is an essential part of the sacrament of Penance.

Catechism #1455-1456

Satisfaction

"Absolution takes away sin, but it does not remedy all the disorders sin has caused. Raised up from sin, the sinner must still recover his full spiritual health by doing something more to make amends for the sin ... It can consist of prayer, an offering, works of mercy, service of neighbor, voluntary self-denial, sacrifices, and above all the patient acceptance of the cross we must bear.

Catechism #1459-1469

Confession and the Gift of Peace

"Jesus came and stood among [his apostles] and said to them: 'Peace be with you. As the Father has sent me, even so I send you ... Receive the Holy Spirit. If you forgive the sins of any, they are forgiven; if you retain the sins of any, they are retained."

John 20:19-23

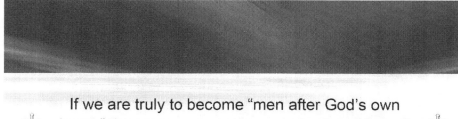

If we are truly to become "men after God's own heart," the mercy we receive, we must practice. It must become magnanimous.

The Superabundant Mercy of God

- "Through the centuries the Church has become ever more aware that Mary, 'full of grace' through God, was redeemed from the moment of her conception. That is what the dogma of the Immaculate Conception confesses" (Catechism #491).

- "Husbands, love your wives, as Christ loved the Church and gave himself up for her ... that she might be holy and without blemish" (Ephesians 5:25-27).

Mercy as the Light to our Path

"The light of divine mercy will illumine the way for the men and women of the third millennium ... this consoling message is addressed above all to those who, afflicted by a particularly harsh trial or crushed by the weight of the sins they committed, have lost all confidence in life and are tempted to give in to despair."

Pope John Paul II

Covenant on the Mercy of God

"I will receive the Sacrament of Reconciliation once each month or immediately upon committing a serious sin. I will manifest the merciful Father by helping my family avoid the occasions of sin and performing one gratuitous act for each member of my family each week."

TMIY

Encountering the Merciful Father

- Receive God's mercy in the Sacrament of Reconciliation (preferably during Holy Week).
- Ask forgiveness of your wife and children for the times you have not lived up to your high calling of husband and father.
- Receive the Eucharist on Easter morning.
- Recite the Magnificat of Mary in praise of the mercy of God.
- Celebrate with family and friends.

Small Group Discussion

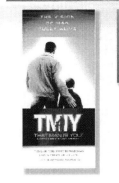

Starter Questions
1. When have you most profoundly experienced the mercy of God?
2. When have you most profoundly offered the mercy of God to another person?

Next Week
Encountering the Good Master

SESSION 25
Encountering the Good Master

That Man is You! is about a personal encounter with Jesus Christ so that Jesus Christ can transform your life.

The Saddest Story in the Gospel (Mark 10:17-22)

- "Good Teacher: what must I do to inherit everlasting life?"
- "You know the commandments."
- "All these I have observed from my youth."
- "Jesus looking upon him loved him, 'You lack one thing: go, sell what you have, and give to the poor, and you will have treasure in heaven; and come, follow me.'"
- "At this saying his countenance fell, and he went away sorrowful."

The Seven Covenants of That Man is You!

1. "I will honor my wedding vows by living in sexual purity."
2. "I will use my money and resources for the formation of other people."
3. "I will give some of my time to God, beginning with Sunday. I will attend Mass together with my family and make the gift of that day to them."
4. "I will elevate my mind to God by spending 15 minutes/day reading Scripture."
5. "I will Practice the Presence of God by receiving Christ in the Eucharist at least one day each week in addition to Sunday."
6. "I will praise God 7 times/day for finding his Hidden Face in those closest to me, especially in my wife and children."
7. "I will go to Confession once each month and perform a gratuitous act for each member of my family each week."

TMIY

A Spiritual Plan of Life

1. *Daily*
- Honor your wedding vows by living in sexual purity (1st Covenant).
- Use money for the formation of family members (2nd Covenant).
- Read Scripture 15 minutes (4th Covenant).
- Praise God seven times (6th Covenant).

2. *Weekly*
- Reclaim Sunday for God and family (3rd Covenant).
- Receive Eucharist in addition to Sunday (5th Covenant).
- Gratuitous act for each member of your family (7th Covenant).

3. *Monthly*
- Receive God's mercy in confession (7th Covenant).

Making it Practical

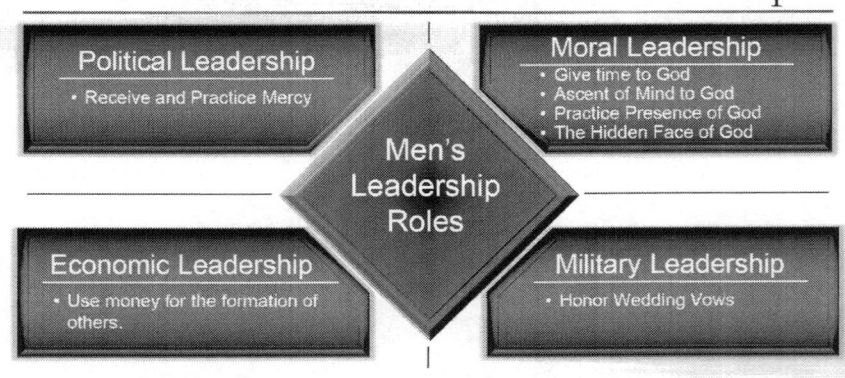

- "A what without a when is a never!"
- We must get practical about integrating these covenants into a way of life.
- The TMIY Mobile App
  - ✓ Delivery of TMIY content.
  - ✓ Integration of 7 steps into a way of life through selection of TMIYs (TiMYs)
  - ✓ Formation of small groups.
- Additional formation available.

The Fulfillment of Authentic Leadership

Political Leadership
- Receive and Practice Mercy

Moral Leadership
- Give time to God
- Ascent of Mind to God
- Practice Presence of God
- The Hidden Face of God

Men's Leadership Roles

Economic Leadership
- Use money for the formation of others.

Military Leadership
- Honor Wedding Vows

I have been asked on many occasions about my own path from trading energy derivatives to my work at Paradisus Dei.

Steve Bollman's Conversion Process

1. **Began reading Spiritual Books**
   - I read 50 spiritual books the first year after my awakening.
   - I necessarily had to significantly curtail my consumption of the media.
   - I was living the Ascent of the Mind to God.
   - I learned to think with the mind of the Church (Covenant with Peter).

2. **Began saying the Rosary**
   - I began to say the Rosary every night.
   - I was living the Covenant with Mary.
   - She was preparing me to receive the superabundant mercy of God.

3. **Participated in the Sacraments in a more Profound Way**
   - I returned to Confession and began going to daily Mass.
   - I was living the Covenant of the Eucharist, which helped me to Practice the Presence of God.

Christ's Three Gifts for your Spiritual Life

1. *St. Peter*
   - "On this rock I will build my church, and the powers of death shall not prevail against it" (Matthew 16:18).
   - "He who hears you hears me" (Luke 10:16).
   - "When you have turned again, strengthen your brethren" (Luke 22:32).

2. *The Blessed Virgin Mary*
   - "Jesus said, 'Woman, behold your son! ... [Disciple], behold your mother!' And, from that hour the disciple took her to his own home" (John 19:26-27).

3. *The Eucharist*
   - "My flesh is food indeed, and my blood is drink indeed. He who eats my flesh and drinks my blood abides in me, and I in him" (John 6:55-56).

Over time God began to reveal his presence within marriage and family life and I began to understand why it is not good for man to be alone.

God's Presence in the Spousal Union

- "Where two or three are gathered in my name, there am I in the midst of them" (Matthew 18:20).

- "Shelly receive this ring as a sign of my love and fidelity. In the name of the Father, and of the Son and of the Holy Spirit" (Marriage Ceremony).

Christ's Presence in Children

- "Whoever receives one such child in my name receives me ... See that you do not despise one of these little ones" (Matthew 18:5, 10).
- "For by His incarnation the Son of God has united Himself in some fashion with every man" (*Gaudium et Spes*, #22).

The Paradise of the Holy Family

[The Holy Family] was a heaven, a paradise on earth, endless delights in this place of grief; it was a glory already begun in the vileness, abjection and lowliness of their life.

Monsieur Jean-Jacques Olier
1608-1657

Making Time for God and Family

- 6:30am – Wake and Morning Prayer
- 7:00am – Breakfast with Family
- 7:30am – Car Pool (pray 15 minutes in car after drop-off)
- 8:15am – Morning Mass
- 9:00am – Begin Work
- 1:00pm – Lunch with Wife
- 1:30pm – Return to work
- 5:30pm – Dinner and Family Time
- 8:30pm – Get Children to Bed
- 9:00pm – Shower
- 9:30pm – Prayer and Reading
- 10:30pm – Time with Wife
- 11:30pm – Bedtime

Finding God within marriage and family life is the foundation upon which Pope John Paul II wished to build the new springtime.

The Vision of a New Springtime

"God is opening before the church the horizons of a humanity more fully prepared for the sowing of the Gospel … I see the dawning of a new missionary age, which will become a radiant day bearing an abundant harvest … As the third millennium of the redemption draws near, God is preparing a great springtime for Christianity."

Redemptoris Missio #3, #92, #86

The "Program" for the Future

"To contemplate the face of Christ, and to contemplate it with Mary, is the 'programme' which I have set before the Church at the dawn of the third millennium, summoning her to put out into the deep on the sea of history with the enthusiasm of the new evangelization."

Ecclesia de Eucaristia, #6

To Contemplate the Face of Christ

- "The shepherds went with haste, and found Mary and Joseph, and the babe lying in a manger. And when they saw it they made known the saying which had been told them concerning this child; and all who heard it wondered at what the shepherds told them. But Mary kept all these things, pondering them in her heart" (Luke 2:16-19).

- "The future of the world and of the Church passes through the family" (Pope John Paul II, Familiaris Consortio, #75).

A Gift for the Family

"I understood that I must lead Christ's Church into this third millennium through suffering … Precisely because the family is threatened, the family is under attack. The Pope has to be attacked, the Pope has to suffer, so that every family and the world may see that there is … a higher Gospel … by which the future is prepared, the third millennium of families."

May 29, 1994

The Grace of the Great Jubilee

"But certainly 'a river of living water' ... has been poured out on the Church. This is the water of the Spirit which quenches thirst and brings new life ... Christ whom we have contemplated and loved bids us to set out once more on our journey ... we can count on the power of the same Holy Spirit who was poured out at Pentecost and who impels us still today to start out anew."

Novo Millennio Ineunte #1, #57

The Transformation of Men

"Behold, I will send you Elijah the prophet before the great and terrible day of the Lord comes. And he will turn the hearts of fathers to their children and the hearts of children to their fathers, lest I come and smite the land with a curse."

Malachi 4:6

The New Springtime is dependent upon men stepping up as husbands and fathers. It is dependent upon you embracing the path set before you.

Small Group Discussion

Starter Questions

1. How are you going to incorporate the Seven Covenants of That Man is You! into a way of life?
2. How can you help bring the message of God's presence in the home to other people?

Next Week
A Man after God's own Heart

A Spiritual Reading List

1. The Bible
2. Confessions of S. Augustine
3. The Cloud of Unknowing
4. Little Flowers of S. Francis
5. Revelations of Divine Love
6. Dialogue of S. Catherine Siena
7. Imitation of Christ
8. Spiritual Exercises S. Ignatius
9. Ascent of Mt. Carmel
10. Interior Castle
11. Introduction to the Devout Life
12. Practice of Presence of God
13. True Devotion to B.V.M.
14. Abandon. to Divine Providence
15. Story of a Soul
16. Catechism of the Catholic Church
17. St. Joseph: The Shadow of the Father
18. Give Me Souls (Don Bosco)
19. Wherever He Goes (Philippe)
20. Immaculate Conception & Holy Spirit
21. Theology of Body (JPII)
22. Theology of History (Ratzinger)
23. True Devotion to Sacred Heart
24. Way of Divine Love
25. Mary and Fathers of Church
26. Woman Clothed with the Sun
27. Dark Night of the Soul
28. Spiritual Canticle
29. Mother Teresa: Come Be My Light
30. Catholic Prophecy (DuPont)

A Secular Reading List

31. The Science of God
32. The Hidden Face of God
33. Why God Won't Go Away
34. How God Changes Your Brain
35. The Male Brain
36. The Female Brain
37. Sex and Cognition
38. The Developing Mind
39. The Shallows: What the Internet is Doing to Our Brains
40. Why We Love
41. Soul Searching
42. The Rise of Christianity
43. The Case for Marriage
44. The Medical Consequences of Loneliness
45. The First Relationship
46. Home Alone America
47. The Social Organization of Sexuality
48. The Estrogen Effect
49. The Greatest Experiment Ever Performed on Women
50. From Good to Great

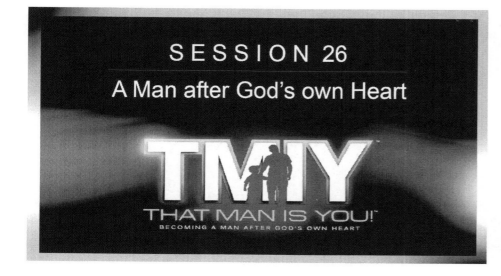

SESSION 26

A Man after God's own Heart

TMIY

THAT MAN IS YOU!™

BECOMING A MAN AFTER GOD'S OWN HEART

What an incredible year! More than anything else, this year has been a journey into the heart of mercy.

A Spiritual Plan of Life

1. **King David Needed Mercy**
   - "Nathan said to David, 'That man is you!'" (2 Samuel 12:7).
2. **King David Encountered God**
   - "Have mercy on me, O God according to thy steadfast love; according to thy abundant mercy blot out my transgressions" (Psalm 51:1).
3. **King David was Transformed**
   - "I have found in David the son of Jesse, a man after my heart, who will do all my will" (Acts 13:22).

My mind returns to the apparitions of Divine Mercy. Pope John Paul II said that they would enlighten the path for our journey through the third millennium of Christianity.

The Divine Mercy Apparitions

- 1905-1938: St. Faustina Kowalska.
- 1931-1938: The Divine Mercy Apparitions of Christ.
- 1931: The vision of the Divine Mercy of Christ image.
- 1931: Request to establish the Feast of Divine Mercy.
- 1935: Receives the Divine Mercy Chaplet.
- 1938: Dies on October 5th.
- 2000: Canonized as the first saint of the new millennium on April 16th.
- 2000: The establishment of the Feast of Divine Mercy is the first liturgical initiative of the new Millennium.
- Chronicled: "Divine Mercy in My Soul – The Diary of St. M. Faustina Kowalska.

The Image of Divine Mercy

"Paint an image according to the pattern you see, with the signature: Jesus, I trust in you. I desire that this image be venerated, first in your chapel, and [then] throughout the world. I promise that the soul that will venerate this image will not perish. I also promise victory over [its] enemies already here on earth, especially at the hour of death. I myself will defend it as My own glory."

Divine Mercy in My Soul, #47-48.

The Abundance of Christ's Mercy

"How very much I desire the salvation of souls ... I want to pour out My divine life into human souls and to sanctify them, if only they were willing to accept My grace. The greatest sinners would achieve great sanctity, if only they would trust in My mercy. The very inner depths of My being are filled to overflowing with mercy, and it is being poured out upon all that I have created. My delight is to act in a human soul and to fill it with My mercy."

Divine Mercy in My Soul, #1784

Trust in Divine Mercy

"To humanity, which at times seems to be lost and dominated by the power of evil, egotism and fear, the risen Lord offers as a gift his love that forgives, reconciles and reopens the spirit to hope. It is love that converts hearts and gives peace. How much need the world has to understand and accept Divine Mercy. Lord, who with [your] Death and Resurrection reveal the love of the Father, we believe in you and with confidence repeat to you today: Jesus, I trust in You, have mercy on us and on the whole world."

April 3, 2005.

We have for you an image of Divine Mercy. Trust in Divine Mercy. Receive Divine Mercy. Spread Divine Mercy. Let it be the light for your path.

You will notice that there are three places on this certificate. Our journey has just begun. There is a man who helps us to understand this journey: St. Joseph. He is the true man after God's heart.

The Humility of St. Joseph

- Does not speak a single word in Scripture.
- Royal line, but is poor.
- Know nothing of past, parents, death.
- Amazingly absent from Church Fathers.
- No major church in Holy Land.
- No major church in Rome.
- 1129: 1st church in west (Bologna)
- 1479: Feast in Universal Church
- 1729: Name added to Litany of Saints.
- 1870: Patron of Universal Church.
- 1962: Name added to Roman Canon.

The Mystery of St. Joseph

- "Joseph, being a just man ... resolved to send Mary away quietly" (Matthew 1:19).
- "The angel Gabriel was sent from God to a city of Galilee named Nazareth, to a virgin betrothed to a man whose name was Joseph" (Luke 1:26-27).
- "And when they saw him they were astonished; and his mother said to him, 'Son, why have you treated us so? Behold, your father and I have been looking for you anxiously' ... and Jesus ... was obedient to them" (Luke 2:48-51).

A Man after God's own Heart

- "When Joseph woke from sleep, he did as the angel of the Lord commanded him" (Matthew 1:24).
- "And he rose and took the child and his mother by night" (Matthew 2:14).
- "And he rose and took the child and his mother, and went to the land of Israel" (Matthew 2:21).
- "Being warned in a dream he withdrew to the district of Galilee" (Matthew 2:22).

The Hidden Face of Christ

- "A virgin betrothed to a man whose name was Joseph" (Luke 1:27).
- "The messenger flies swiftly to the spouse, in order to remove every attachment to a human marriage from God's spouse. He does not take the Virgin away from Joseph but simply restores her to Christ ... Christ, then, takes his own bride; he does not steal someone else's" (St. Peter Chrysologus).

The Revelation of the Father

- "Your father and I have been looking for you anxiously ... and Jesus ... was obedient to them" (Luke 2:48-51).
- "The admirable St. Joseph was given to the earth to express the adorable perfection of God the Father in a tangible way. In his person alone, he bore the beauties of God the Father ... one saint alone is destined to represent God the Father" (Fr. Andrew Doze).

The world needs more men like St. Joseph. We must learn to follow his path.

The Path of That Man is You!

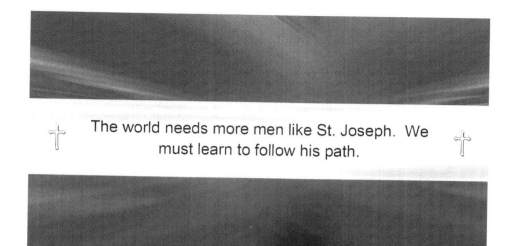

An Entry into the Mystery of St. Joseph

- Year 1: We seek to become a Man after God's own Heart by living in union with God the Father.
- Year 2: We seek to take the next step and to learn how to discern the will of God in our lives.
- Year 3: We seek to become the Hidden Face of Christ, especially to our spouse.
- Year 4: We seek to become the Revelation of the Father, especially to our own children.

Year 2: The Spirit of Nazareth

In the Spirit of Nazareth, you will discover:
- A practical guide for evaluating the current status of your spiritual life.
- The time honored means for winning the spiritual battle and discovering a peace "not of this world."
- The practical means for developing a prayer life that puts you into communion with God.
- The true source of the struggles in the spiritual life, and its manifestation in competing brain systems encouraging you to be a saint or locking you in a life of sin.

Year 2: The Spirit of Nazareth

- The means for hearing God's voice and discerning his will in your life.
- A step-by-step guide to developing a "spiritual plan of life" that enables you to make true progress in your spiritual life.
- The consistent guidance given by the Magisterium (Popes) for the past 50 years regarding the spiritual significance of our times.
- The grace being offered families to experience the love, peace and joy found within the Holy Family

We have just begun our journey. Have no fear about what lies ahead. We have the perfect man for our guide.

Faith for the Journey

"Do not be afraid of Christ! He takes nothing away, and He gives you everything. When we give ourselves to Him, we receive a hundredfold in return. Yes, open, open wide the doors to Christ-- and you will find true life. Amen."

Pope Benedict XVI
April 24, 2005

A Prayer to St. Joseph

" To you, O Blessed Joseph, we come in our trials, and ... we confidently ask your patronage ... O most provident guardian of the Holy Family, defend the chosen children of Jesus Christ ... dispel the evil of falsehood and sin ... gracious assist us from heaven in our struggle with the powers of darkness ... Shield each one of us by your constant protection, so that, supported by your example and your help, we may be able to live a virtuous life, to die a holy death, and to obtain eternal happiness in heaven. Amen. "

Pope Leo XIII
Quamquam Pluries (1889)

Small Group Discussion

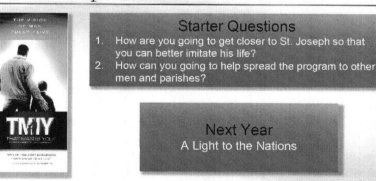

Starter Questions

1. How are you going to get closer to St. Joseph so that you can better imitate his life?
2. How can you going to help spread the program to other men and parishes?

Next Year
A Light to the Nations

Suggested Additional Reading

Secular
1. The Case for Marriage – Linda Waite and Christine Gallagher
2. The Index of Leading Cultural Indicators – William J. Bennett
3. Children, Adolescents and the Media – Victor C. Strasburger
4. Good to Great – Jim Collins
5. A Treatise on the Family – Gary S. Becker
6. The Rise of Christianity – Rodney Stark
7. Fewer: How the new Demography of Depopulation will Shape our Future – Ben J. Wattenburg
8. Father Facts – National Fatherhood Initiative – Wade F. Horn and Tom Sylvester
9. Soft Porn Plays Hardball – Judith A. Reismann
10. The Medical Consequences of Loneliness – James J. Lynch
11. The High Price of Materialism – Tim Kasser

Religious
1. Mother Teresa: Come Be My Light – Brian Kolodiejchuck
2. Memory and Identity – Pope John Paul II
3. Joseph of Nazareth – Federico Suarez
4. Fatima, Russia and the Pope – Timothy Tindal-Robertson
5. Confessions – St. Augustine
6. Crossing the Threshold of Hope – Pope John Paul II
7. The Voyage to Lourdes – Alexis Carrel/Stanley L. Jaki
8. The Story of a Soul – St. Therese of Lisieux
9. Lectio Divina and the Practice of Teresian Prayer – Institute of Carmelite Studies
10. Give Me Souls: The Life of Don Bosco – Father Peter Lappin
11. Wherever He Goes – Fr. Marie Dominique Philippe
12. The Practice of the Presence of God – Brother Lawrence of the Resurrection
13. Divine Mercy in My Soul – St. Faustina Kowalska

Church Documents
1. The Catechism of the Catholic Church
2. Compendium of the Social Doctrine of the Church
3. Dives in Misericordia – Pope John Paul II
4. Novo Millennio Ineunte, Pope John Paul II
5. Redemptoris Hominis - Pope John Paul II
6. Gratissimam Sane – Pope John Paul II

THAT MAN IS YOU!

Made in the USA
Lexington, KY
27 September 2016